# THE JAGUAR STORY

*Automotive Books by* JOSEPH H. WHERRY

Economy Car Blitz
Antique and Classic Cars
The M.G. Story
The Jaguar Story
The Alfa-Romeo Story (in preparation)
Automobiles of the World (in preparation)

# THE
# JAGUAR
## STORY

### BY JOSEPH H. WHERRY

*Chilton's Sebring Series*

## CHILTON BOOK COMPANY
Philadelphia   New York   London

*To my son,* JOE

# *Foreword*

DURING the arid period between the two World Wars, we of the sports car clan in the United States were reduced to driving some very unromantic iron. High performance domestic automobiles consisting mostly of Model J and A Duesenbergs, DV32 Stutzes and the like, were way beyond our slim pocketbooks, and imported Bugattis, Lagondas and Bentleys were for millionaires only. The average enthusiast relied on the good old Model T Ford block and chassis and cluttered it up with Morton & Brett-supplied racing equipment, and on the famous Gaston Chevrolet "Frontenac" overhead cam conversions. Harry Miller's carburetors were a must.

In Europe, the situation was not much better. The impecunious enthusiast in France could pick up a battered Amilcar or a Salmson Cycle-Car and hope for the best, whereas in Britain the M.G. Midget was about all there was available on the economy bill-of-fare. It was during this period that Bill Lyons (now Sir William

Lyons) had the bright idea of supplementing his "Swallow" motorcycle sidecar business with sleek looking sports cars assembled from well-known, reliable English components. In short order, he captured the market that was awaiting a wide-awake manufacturer who could supply a quality car at a bargain basement price.

My first confrontation with a Jaguar took place in Connecticut late in 1939 when a friend lent me an SS100 sports roadster to throw around the local back roads. I was fresh from a Briggs Cunningham-owned, supercharged SSK Mercedes, which left me with various pains and aches. The springs in this monster from Stuttgart were, in my opinion, for show purposes only. Imagine my surprise when I took the wheel of the SS100 to find its acceleration just as hairy as that of the blown Mercedes, with the difference that it rode and steered like a sports automobile. All this, I was informed, at a fraction of the cost of the Rolls Royce Bentley, which it emulated very closely.

The post World War II success of the Jaguar firm is well known to all. From its debut at the London Show in 1948, the XK120 moved into the forefront as a competition sports car and its descendants covered themselves with glory at Sebring, Le Mans and other international circuits . . . But still you hear the old refrain no matter where you go: "How can Jaguar offer so much at such a low price?" This volume covers the subject most expertly and provides many an answer to the success of the Jaguar.

ALEC ULLMAN
President, Automobile Racing Club of Florida

# Acknowledgments

THE author wishes to express his sincere appreciation to those who have so kindly lent their cooperation: J. A. Graham and his staff at Jaguar Cars Limited in Coventry and John Dugdale in New York; Al Arth, Wayne Greer, George McNabb and Tom Johnson of British Motor Car Distributors, Inc., in San Francisco; Ed Fitzpatrick of Santa Rosa British Cars in Santa Rosa; the many owners of Jaguar variants who allowed the author to photograph their cars; John Lyon Reid for lending photos of his lovely S.S. 100 Jaguar; Miles L. Brubacher for lending several precious photographs of his C-type in its original Le Mans form; my son Joseph E. G. Wherry for valuable assistance; and loving thanks to my wife, Bettye, for her invaluable help in proof-reading and typing.

A special greeting, too, to all lovers of that "different breed of cat."

JOSEPH H. WHERRY

# Contents

*Specifications* follow each chapter for the models contained respectively.

# THE JAGUAR STORY

# 1

## Sidecars, Swallows and Jaguars

WHEN William Lyons was born in 1901 in Blackpool, England, his parents quite naturally thought that the lad would one day take over his father's piano business. By the time his formal education was completed at Arnold House, it was obvious that his interests were elsewhere—William had become addicted to motorcycles. Fortunately, contact with motorcars eventually won him away from cycles.

Lyons's industrial perseverance, design skill and contributions to the serious problems faced by his country during and after World War II were rewarded by Queen Elizabeth in 1956 when, after three decades of devotion to automotive science, he was honored with knighthood. As this is written, Sir William has specialized in cars for forty years and is still in active leadership of Jaguar Cars Ltd. and its subsidiary companies, Coventry Climax, Daimler, Guy Motors, and others. In August, 1966, he merged his interests with The British Motor Corporation.

In 1956, Jaguar Cars Limited was honored by a royal visit. Her Majesty Queen Elizabeth II and Sir William Lyons enjoy a pleasant chat about a Type D. (*Jaguar Cars Ltd.*)

The bloodlines of Jaguar cars have been the every-day concern—the life as it were—of William Lyons whose first business venture was the manufacture of motorcycle sidecars, a far cry from the magnificent motor cars bearing the marque Jaguar.

*Sidecars for Motorcycles*

In 1920 Lyons met William Walmsley, a young manu-facturer of well designed sidecars. Impressed with them Lyons purchased a Walmsley rig and the two men soon became close friends. Lyons suggested that he'd like to get into the business—he had a natural talent for design —and Walmsley agreed to take him on. By joining forces they felt they could produce as many as eight or ten sidecars each week. A partnership was formed when Lyons became 21 years of age and the Swallow Sidecar Company Limited was organized with borrowed capital of £1000. The year was 1922. The organization that became Jaguar was on its way.

Larger facilities were obtained immediately and several workers were hired. Soon the two Williams were turning out clean-lined Swallow sidecars of high quality with distinctive hexagon cross-sections, electric lights, and comfortable seats with plenty of legroom. The last has always been a feature of Swallow sidecars.

By 1926 these sidecars were widely known and liked, but increasingly, automobiles were attracting young men and motorcycle popularity was waning.

The partners decided to try their hand at selling to automobile drivers, many of whom were seeking cars

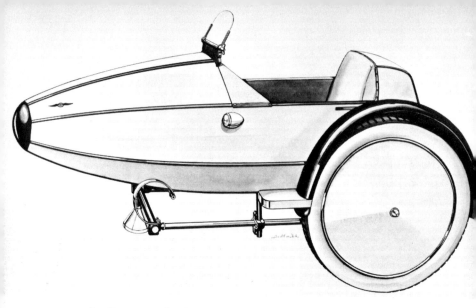

It all started with borrowed money, enthusiasm, and motorcycle side-cars. (*Jaguar Cars Ltd.*)

with distinctive styling. Lyons was rapidly becoming the creative half of the partnership. His ability in design and in merchandising soon vaulted him to the business leadership of the enterprise. In the summer of 1926, larger premises were found on Cocker Street, Blackpool, and that autumn, the first Swallow wood-framed, coach-built body was bolted onto the stock chassis of a little Austin Seven car.

### Swallow Coachwork on Many Popular Chassis

The diminutive Austin Seven—the "Seven" stood for the taxable horsepower—was minimal automotive trans-

In 1926, this modest works in Blackpool, England, housed the firm that became Jaguar. (*Jaguar Cars Ltd.*)

portation to say the most. The 747.5 cc. engine had four tiny cylinders and magneto ignition, and was rated at 13 bhp.* Theoretically, the powerplant was able to move the "Seven" at about 45 mph driving through a three speed, non-synchromesh transmission.

The Austin Company had gained fame producing the sporting "Brooklands" Seven model with a guaranteed top speed of 70 mph. But the run-of-the-mill Seven chassis, beneath the Swallow coachwork, had a serious weak point: the 1⅛-inch-diameter crankshaft had just two main bearings—one in each end of the block. Thus,

* Brake horsepower.

it was fairly commonplace for the hardworking crank-shaft to break at sustained road speeds. Speed, however, was not the objective of Austin Seven buyers, nor was it the aim of the eager customers taken with the pleasant lines of the first Austin-Swallows—fetching little two-seaters with narrow cycle fenders, those in front turning with the wheels. Austin-Swallow drivers bought style and the inexpensive prestige associated with distinctive, custom built vehicles.

The principal change in the otherwise stark interior was a rather well instrumented dash panel, and the steering wheel was raked slightly lower to conform to the decreased overall height. For £175—about $850 in those years—the customer got his money's worth and what he wanted, a zippy looking motor vehicle that appeared faster than it was. For another 10 pounds, the buyer could have a detachable hardtop that was hinged for easier entrance.

Within a few weeks Lyons offered another Swallow, one with a long nose, a V-shaped windshield and a dash panel of mahogany. Based upon a Morris Cowley chassis, only a handful of Morris-Swallows were built because Cecil Kimber at the Morris Garages in Oxford had first call upon Morris chassis for his growing line of M. G. cars. Despite the small numbers produced, the refined lines of the Morris-Swallow attracted customers. In 1927, the Austin-Swallow succeeded it, featuring a variety of dual-tone paint schemes, full fenders and running boards, the stylish V-shaped windshield, and a bustle-like bulge to the posterior smacking a bit of the "torpedo" bodies of some of the larger and more expensive "sport-ing lorries" of the twenties. In answer to customer

Austin Seven plus Swallow coachwork became the Austin-Swallow economy custom car.
(*British Motor Corp.*)

For a few pounds more, the customer could have a two-tone color scheme on his Austin-Swallow saloon in 1928. (*Jaguar Cars Ltd.*)

demands, there were bumpers fore and aft. A small, adjustable roof ventilator topped off the custom innovations designed by William Lyons. In the same year, the firm's name was changed to Swallow-Sidecar & Coachbuilding Company Ltd.

By 1928, the demand for the Austin-based Swallow was sufficient to convince Austin to deliver fifty chassis at a time. Around a dozen cars and sidecars were being built every week and orders again indicated the need for larger facilities. Accordingly in November of 1928, Swallow picked up and moved to Coventry, the center of the British automobile industry. By this time Lyons was managing director and the decision had been made to emphasize the manufacture of automobile bodies.

The Austin-Swallow continued to be popular at home, and even caught the eye of foreign royalty—a purple and black model was delivered to the Sultan of Perak. Special closed coachwork was built upon the Fiat 609A (990 cc.) and the Swift Ten chassis (1190 cc.) from 1929 to 1931. More than 200 of the Fiat and Swift-Swallows were built and sold. Sporting Specials were built during 1931-1933 on the Wolseley Hornet chassis. With its husky overhead camshaft, 1271 cc., six-cylinder powerplant, the Wolseley-Swallow open two-seater was capable of 70 mph and without doubt whetted Lyons's appetite for fast sports cars.

The best-selling Swallow Special by 1930, however, was on the Standard Big Nine chassis, Lyons's version of this 4-cylinder 1287 cc. car having been introduced at Swallow's own stand at the London Show in the fall of 1929. With an overall height of 68 inches, the Standard-Swallow Big Nine was an impressive, four-seater sedan

Austin-Swallow saloons and roadsters under construction in the Foleshill plant in 1929.

(*Jaguar Cars Ltd.*)

Skilled coach-builders hand-fabricated the body frames in the Swallow works about 1929-30. On the left are saloon bodies; on the right, roadster coachwork for Austin Seven small cars. (*Jaguar Cars Ltd.*)

with wire wheels and a distinctive, V-shaped radiator
grille heavily plated in chrome. This grille design
showed up a year or so later on the S.S. Swallow cars, the
first to bear the firm's name as a recognized make in its
own right.

The Standard-Swallow was a sensation. In 1930, the
firm name changed again, this time to Swallow Coachbuilding Company Limited. The die was cast: William
Lyons was preparing to build his own cars. First, however, an event took place which convinced Lyons that
six cylinders were the best basis for quality cars. Early
in 1931 Swallow obtained a 109-inch-wheelbase Standard
Ensign chassis powered by a rugged, 6-cylinder engine

Quality coachwork by Swallow on the 1931–33 Wolseley Hornet chassis.
*(Jaguar Cars Ltd.)*

having a crankshaft with seven main bearings and a displacement of 2054 cc. The long 106.6 mm. stroke gave high torque and smoothness at low speeds. The bore was 65.5 mm. and the output was 48 bhp at 3600 rpm.

## S.S.I, Ancestor of the Modern Jaguars

This new Standard-Swallow Sixteen (this figure indicating its taxable horsepower) attained a shade over 60 mph and, at £275, put Lyons in the medium-quality, family-car business. It probably inspired his own automobile development program, the fruits of which were introduced the following fall at the 1931 London Show. The star of the Swallow works display was the S.S.I, a cycle-fendered saloon without running boards that featured two-plus-two seating inside a very low, rakish body just 55 inches high. The ash, wood-framed body was sheathed with steel panels and the fenders were steel of a heavier gauge. The price for such a high quality car was unbelievable—£310. The S.S.I was truly the car for enthusiasts—and they loved it.

Though the unmodified engine was the proven 2054 cc. powerplant of the Standard Sixteen, the chassis was designed by Lyons and his staff. Underslung at the front and rear, the frame was of sturdy welded box sections. Stock Standard Sixteen cam-and-lever steering and front and rear axles were used but the wheelbase was increased to 112 inches, 3 inches more than that of the Standard-Swallow. Semi-elliptic leaf springs and Hartford lever-type shock absorbers were used all around.

The rakish S.S.I of late 1931 set the pattern for a long line of original sporting machines.

*(Jaguar Cars Ltd.)*

The use of "proprietary components"—sub-assemblies and major assemblies purchased outside the works—was a long established practice on both sides of the Atlantic, the difference being that British car makers more readily admitted that they did not fabricate every single item. Swallow, therefore, openly used the stock Standard Sixteen 4-speed transmission which had reasonably close ratios. This transmission, teamed with the 48 bhp Standard six-cylinder engine, gave the S.S.I a 65-70 mph top speed. Third gear provided a useful and honest 50 mph. The rear axle ratio of 4.66 to 1 was moderately high. Acceleration to 60 mph could be attained in about 26 seconds, fair for the time. Cable-operated, Bendix mechanical brakes and Rudge-Whitworth wire wheels completed the first chassis originally conceived by Swallow.

The meaning of the designation "S.S." has long been the subject of controversy among Swallow buffs. Some have contended that the letters signified "Standard-Swallow." Nothing could be farther from the truth because, except for the engine and the customary "proprietary parts," the S.S.I was a Swallow creation from the frame, built to Lyons's designs by a specialist manufacturer, to the Swallow body and fittings. Neither did "S.S." mean Super Sports as some have conjectured. More than likely "S.S." stood for Swallow Sports because the S.S.I was a marque in its own right and was recognized as such by *The Autocar* in February, 1932.

If the inspired exterior styling caused the blood of the sporting fraternity to tingle, the furniture-quality, "Vaumol"-leather-upholstered, individual front and occasional rear seats, and the luxuriously appointed in-

terior had the same effect on others of discriminating
tastes. A full complement of sports car instruments was
set in oval dials on a facia panel of polished sycamore
wood and the window surrounds of the front-opening
doors were hand-crafted to match. The non-bucket front
seats, with adjustable backrests, were designed to seat
three adults "occasionally" while the rear seat was
suggested "for juvenile passengers." The winding
windows were equipped with rain shields at the tops
while the top-hinged windshield was fitted with dual
electric wipers and could be opened "to any desired
position." The windshield closed tightly on a rubber,
water-tight beading. Underslung, the frame was advertised as assuring "Ample headroom for the tallest
passenger." A large, sliding "sunshine" panel was set
in the steel roof and the separate "Continental" style
luggage trunk was covered with grained leather-like ma-
terial. The trunk lid had heavy chromed hinges and a
sturdy lock. The spare wheel was concealed in the
luggage "boot."

Several color schemes provided relief from the generally dull hues of most contemporary English cars.
Though the 2-litre engine did not provide quite the
performance of the Type 18/80 M.G., an exemplary
competitive vehicle for those requiring distinctive
transport, the S.S.I was some £235 less costly.

Nevertheless, there were demands for more power and
before the end of 1932 the Standard Twenty engine
of 2552 cc. was made optional on order. Bored out to
75 mm. without change in stroke and with an alloy
head, the larger 60 bhp powerplant enabled the per-
formance-conscious S.S.I owner to achieve 75-80 mph

In remarkable, near original condition, this 1934 S.S.I will be restored by owner, attorney Ronald Sullivan. (*Author's photo*)

with ease and to hold his head as high as the stylishly low overall height would permit.

For the 1933 season the S.S.I underwent a moderate restyling. The seasoned-hardwood, coach-type body was lengthened to seat four adults. While the body was longer, the styling was scarcely touched nor was the narrow V-grille with its vertical chrome strips. Only two doors were offered, but the overall appearance was altered greatly by fully balanced, gracefully swept fenders, the front members incorporating running boards as they flaired aft. The long, low look was

Sullivan's S.S.I displays its original, pleated-leather upholstery; note divided rear seat. (*Author's photo*)

The short remote control gear change lever was located well aft in S.S.I. Note wood trim around windows. (*Author's photo*)

Six-cylinder, L-head engines of two sizes were offered in the S.S.I of 1934. This 2.7-litre unit has served faithfully since new. (*Author's photo*)

enhanced by an improved, longer chassis giving 119 inches to the wheelbase and increasing the overall length to 186. Either the 2 or 2½-litre, L-head engine was available, with the latter predominating.

During 1932, the first full year of S.S.I production, 776 cars were built. Henleys, a large London distributor, took the majority. In 1933, production nearly doubled. Even youngsters were envious of their elders and some-

Solid front axle, semi-elliptic springs and lever type friction snubbers of the S.S.I are shown here. (*Author's photo*)

time in 1932 the English firm of Meccano, toy makers par excellence, produced a perfectly scaled miniature of the S.S.I as an early offering in the still-famed Dinky Toys series. (If scores of thousands of readers yearn for an S.S.I, perhaps Meccano might be persuaded to bring back this elegant long-nosed sports carriage in miniature again. Then all of us Jaguar fans could own an S.S.I Swallow.)

Leatherette-topped coachwork and very low lines make Sullivan's 1934 S.S.I fit into modern styling scheme. (*Author's photo*)

A 1933-34 S.S.I saloon in its prime.

(*Jaguar Cars Ltd.*)

*S.S.II, Elegance with Four Cylinders*

William Lyons did not rest on the popularity of the S.S.I but quickly brought out the S.S.II early in 1932 at the astonishingly low price of £210. The styling of the coach-built body was nearly exactly like that of its larger relative with the exception of the radiator grille which was enameled rather than chrome-plated. The S.S.II owed more to Standard than did S.S.I, the 89½ inch wheelbase chassis being that of the Standard Little Nine, although to achieve the long, low lines, the proprietary frame was much modified by Swallow. Overall length was approximately 142 inches. Using the 1052 cc., Standard Nine, L-head engine of 28 bhp, the little S.S.II had a top speed of 60 mph, reached in about 35 seconds, and could be scarcely distinguished from the S.S.I at a distance. Two adults could be accommodated in the front, leather-covered, bucket seats while smaller "juveniles" occupied the rear. For the 1933 model year, the wheelbase and length were increased to 91 and 144 inches respectively and, in 1934, to 104 and 168 inches. Saloon and four-seater open Tourer models were popular with improved engines displacing 1343 or 1608.5 cc. and developing 32 and 38 bhp. With the larger powerplant, the S.S.II Tourer did 84 mph. Several police departments bought the first of these. Production of the S.S.II—drop-head and fixed-top coupe, saloon and tourer models—continued well into 1936, gradually giving ground to the new "Jaguar" range.

The 1933–34 S.S.II was smaller, had four cylinders and styling like that of larger S.S.I.

*(Jaguar Cars Ltd.)*

*Faster S.S.I Tourers, Saloons and Streamliners*

Lyons had a distaste for exterior change for the mere sake of change. When he changed things they were improvements, whether seen or unseen. For instance, the 1931-1932 S.S.I had a tendency to overheat, so the longer, 119-inch-wheelbase 1933-1935 models were provided with increased radiator capacity. Also, a tighter firewall kept obnoxious engine odors from the cockpit, a frequent 1932 complaint.

When a four-seater Tourer was introduced into the S.S.I series late in 1933, a team was entered by the works in the Alpine Trials, but without success. In the 1934 event, though, the team took 3rd place. In the same year an improved 2663.7 cc. engine gave 68 bhp and 77 mph. Additional body models were also developed, the four-window Saloon being particularly attractive. Enthusiasts were further enticed late in 1934 by an "Airline" model, a streamlined, limited-production, 80-mph variant fitted with the 2663.7 cc. engine. A somewhat bulbously rounded tail-end and a spare wheel in each front fender added to the Airline's distinctive lines. The interior was like that of the Coupe.

By early 1935, the Swallow plant was fully occupied with production of S.S. cars exclusively, no custom bodies being placed on other makers' chassis. The sidecar portion of the business had become a separate subsidiary and the firm name became S.S. Cars Limited. William Walmsley left to make house trailers, and the

In 1934, William Lyons introduced the four window version of the sensational S.S.I.

*(Jaguar Cars Ltd.)*

The limited production S.S.I "Airline" model of 1934 gave owner 80 mph.

*(Jaguar Cars Ltd.)*

public was offered stock in the reorganized company which William Lyons continued to head. "Jaguar" was selected after lengthy deliberations as the name of the future cars, and production neared the 2000-per-year mark, a respectable production figure for a quality car manufacturer in pre-World War II years.


## The S.S.90 Two-Seater Sports Car

The big news of the 1935 model year, however, was the S.S.90 sports two-seater. Powered by the old 2663.7 cc. L-head engine, only fifty units were made on a 104-inch-wheelbase, box-section frame designed by Lyons. Underslung in the rear, the S.S.90 terminated either with a sloping tail or a slab-type fuel tank. It was the ambition of Lyons to market the S.S.90 as a 100-mph sports machine, but the performance fell short of the mark. The price of £395 was right but, since the faithful 2663.7 cc. engine urgently needed overhead valves, the lovely two-seater was short-lived. In reality a transitional car, the S.S.90 paved the way for the next four years during which a 100 mph sports car was to be the top cat of the new litter. The marque S.S. Jaguar became synonomous with high-performance sports cars and family sedans with genuine sporting characteristics.

In 1935, the S.S.90 sports car was indicative of things to come.

(*Jaguar Cars Ltd.*)

# SPECIFICATIONS  Chapter 1

|  | S.S. I for '32 | S.S. I for late '32 | S.S. I for '33 | S.S. I for '34–'35 |
|---|---|---|---|---|
| Cylinders & Valves | 6 L-head | 6 L-head | 6 L-head | 6 L-head |
| Bore, Stroke (mm.) | 65.5 x 101.6 | 75 x 101.6 | 65.5 x 101.6<br>75   x 101.6 | 65.5 x 106 |
| Displacement (cc.) | 2054 | 2552 | 2054 or 2552 | 2143 |
| Compression ratio | approx. 5.75 | approx. 5.75 | approx. 5.75 | approx. 6.00 |
| Carburetors | 1 Solex | 1 SU or RAG | 1 SU or RAG | 1 RAG (2 in '35) |
| Brake horse-power @ RPM | 48 @ 3600 | 62 @ 3600 | 48 @ 3600 or 62 @ 3600 | 53 |
| Gear speeds | 4 | 4 | 4 | 4 |
| Gear ratios |  |  |  |  |
| Rear axle ratio | 4.66 | 4.66 | 4.66 | 4.75 4.50 in '35 |
| Length overall (inches) | 174 | 174 | 186 | 186 |
| Width overall | 60 | 60 | 63 | 65.5 |
| Height overall | 55 | 55 | 55 | 55 |
| Tires | 18 x 4.75 18 x 5.50 | 18 x 5.50 | 18 x 5.50 | 18 x 5.50 16 x 5.50 |
| Wheelbase | 112 | 112 | 119 | 119 |
| Tread, front<br>"      rear | 49<br>49 | 49<br>49 | 51<br>51 | 53.5<br>53.5 |
| Curb weight (approx.) | 2400 | 2400 | 2650 | 2900 |

*NOTE:* Engines, etc., as detailed above are for model-year seasons; there was overlapping availability as text explains.

| | S.S. I<br>for '34–'35 | S.S. II<br>for '32–'33 | S.S. II<br>for '34,<br>early '36 | S.S. 90<br>(1935 only) |
|---|---|---|---|---|
| Cylinders &<br>Valves | 6 L-head | 4 L-head | 4 L-head | 6 L-head |
| Bore, Stroke<br>(mm.) | 73 x 106 | 60.25 x 88 | 63.5 x 106<br>69.5 x 106 | 73 x 106 |
| Displacement<br>(cc.) | 2663.7 | 1052 | 1343<br>1608.5 | 2663.7 |
| Compression<br>ratio | approx. 6.00 | | | |
| Carburetors | 1 RAG<br>(2 for '35) | 1 Solex '32<br>1 SU or<br>RAG '33 | 1 RAG '34<br>2 RAG '35–'36 | 2 RAG |
| Brake horse-<br>power @<br>RPM | 68 @ 3800<br>(approx.) | 28 @ 4000 | 32 @ 4000<br>38 @ 4000 | variously<br>quoted as<br>68 to 90 bhp |
| Gear speeds | 4 | 3 in '32; 4–'33 | 4 | 4 |
| Gear ratios | | | | |
| Rear axle<br>ratio | 4.25 | 4.66 in '33 | 5.29 | 4.5 |
| Length overall<br>(inches) | 186* | 142<br>144 for '33 | 168 | 150 |
| Width overall | 65.5 | 54 | 55 | 63 |
| Height overall | 55* | 54 | 54 | |
| Tires | 18 x 5.50 | 18 x 4.75 | 18 x 4.75 | 18 x 5.50 |
| Wheelbase | 119 | 89.5<br>91 for '33 | 104 | 104 |
| Tread, front<br>" rear | 53.5*<br>53.5* | 44.25<br>44.25 | 46.5<br>46.5 | 54<br>54 |
| Curb weight<br>(approx.) | 2900 | 2625 | 2200 up | 2600 |

* From 1935: Length 183.5; Height 56.5; Tread 53.6 inches.

# 2

# The Swallows Become
# S.S. Jaguars

WITH the approach of autumn in 1935, Lyons's automobile enterprise had entered a new era and the buying public was well aware of the corporate changes that had taken place. Assured that the popular S.S.I and S.S.II series would continue without change, at least for a while, and well briefed by England's superbly alert motoring press that the newly named "S.S. Jaguar" cars would be logical improvements of the old S.S. lines, the public thronged to the London Show in October, 1935, to view the 1936 models.

The signs proclaiming S.S. Cars Ltd. only served to heighten interest. Swallows, as a marque, were no more. All efforts of the works would henceforth be devoted to cars, the motorcycle sidecar business having become a separate and independently operated subsidiary. If some suspected that the S.S.I and II series were to be not long for the motoring world, all concern was dispensed with due to pledges—well kept as matters developed—that parts and service would be continued

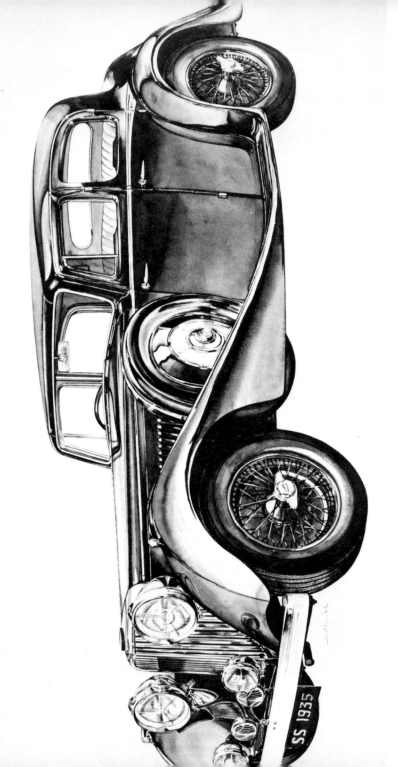

In October, 1935, Lyons introduced his first 4-door sedan, the lovely S.S. Jaguar.

*(Jaguar Cars Ltd.)*

for the several thousand cars in use throughout England and the continent.

By late 1935, the site of S.S. Cars Ltd. in Foleshill, Coventry, covered thirteen acres. Although some component parts and assemblies were "bought in" from proprietary suppliers, all major parts of Lyons's cars were designed in his own engineering laboratories and thoroughly tested there as well. It is safe to say that the only non-Jaguar parts in the 1936 cars were the ignition system components by Lucas, the Girling mechanical brakes, the wheels and Dunlop tires, Smiths instruments, windshield wipers, door locks, and the like. The 1936 range was all S.S. Jaguar and any resemblance to Standards, and others, was as coincidental as such instances in competitive cars.

The plant's main output for 1936 continued to be closed cars, but for the first time, four doors rather than two heralded a change to full adult accommodations. Though built with the family man in mind, the cars still offered sporting character and performance. The two-door S.S. models of older design were available in unchanged layout for the sports car purists who wanted no "family lorry" compromises.

The new 1936 line signaled a most noteworthy structural and engineering change: henceforth, all closed models featured all-steel bodies. Wood-framed coachwork was a thing of the past except in the case of the new S.S. Jaguar sports cars. The natural and expected outgrowth of the S.S.90—a disappointment with respect to performance—the top star of the works range was to retain the wood-framed coachwork throughout its production life.

*The Magnificent S.S.100 Jaguars*

William Lyons was still determined to have a 100-mph sports car and the low production S.S.90 was a good basis to build upon. Refinements in tuning, increasing the compression ratio to 7.6 to 1, a virtual redesign of the 6-cylinder engine block, and improving the gearing and rear axle ratios, resulted in a new overhead-valve powerplant of 2663.7 cc. and a power train that was uniquely Jaguar's own. The crankshaft had seven main bearings, was extremely rigid and precisely counterbalanced. The finned-aluminum crankcase cooled more efficiently, held 10 quarts of oil under 40-60 pounds pressure, and was serviced by an external filter on the lower left side of the block.

At a power peak of 4600 rpm, 102 bhp was developed. Rubber-based engine mounts dampened vibration. The clutch was a single-plate, dry-disc type and the gearbox had synchromesh on top, third and second gears.

The classic body was nearly identical in external appearance to that of the S.S.90 and was fabricated of aluminum over a coach-built frame of seasoned ash. The gracefully shaped fenders were also of aluminum. The cockpit was quite spacious for a sports car. Top-grain cowhide over bucket seats and a walnut facia containing a host of round-dialed Smiths instruments including a tachometer added a note of luxury. There was space for luggage behind the seats beneath the tonneau cover. A short-throw gear shift lever, a fly-off,

The first models of the fabulous S.S.100 Jaguar have 2½-litre engines. Note the huge brake drums.

(*Jaguar Cars Ltd.*)

S.S.100 bodies were aluminum-paneled over coach-built frames of seasoned ash. This 3½-litre model belongs to architect John Lyon Reid, has been exhibited in Briggs Cunningham's museum. *(Courtesy John Lyon Reid)*

racing-type handbrake, and a man-sized steering wheel with a large cross-sectioned wood rim symbolized "Super Sports," which is what the initials "S.S." *could* have meant when coupled with "Jaguar" on the emblem. As in other fine British cars, a well-stocked set of tools was supplied and most S.S.100 drivers knew how to use them.

The frame was of two parallel, longitudinal box sections of very rigid construction, swept steeply upward over the front axle and beneath the rear springs. Front

This spacious cockpit restored to original condition graces one of the finest S.S.100 Jaguars in existence. (*Courtesy John Lyon Reid*)

and rear, the springs were semi-elliptics with laminated leaves. Shackles were used with the exception of the rear ends of the front springs which were machined flat and mounted through pivoting trunnions, the latter to reduce side sway to a minimum. Shock absorbers, fore and aft, were adjustable, hydraulic-lever types made by Luvax. Many existing S.S.100 Jaguars employ Hartford friction snubbers as replacements. The front axle was of the beam type with an H-section, and the Burman-Douglas worm gear steering was light and quick, providing a turning circle diameter of just 36 feet—quite respectable for a 104-inch-wheelbase car in 1936 and maneuverable by today's compact car standards. Total weight with oil and fuel was approximately 2600 pounds.

Dave Garroway's S.S.100 Jaguar has been modified with alligator skin on the instrument facia panel. (*Author's photo*)

The upward sweep of the frame over front axle can be seen in this photo of Garroway's S.S.100 Jaguar displayed in the 1953 International Motor Sports Show in New York City. (*Author's Photo*)

Wartime "blitz" damage is responsible for lack of running boards on John Lyon Reid's superb S.S.100 Jaguar which has the 3½-litre engine. (*Courtesy John Lyon Reid*)

The S.S.100 Jaguar was a top competitor in hill climbs as well as races in late thirties.

(*Jaguar Cars Ltd.*)

With 18-inch, center-locking Dunlop wire wheels, there were approximately 7 inches of road clearance making the S.S.100 a good mount for trials and hill-climbs. Since the fuel tank held 17 Imperial gallons (about 20 U.S. gallons), the 18-20 miles per gallon on the highway allowed considerable travel between re-fueling stops. At 65-mph-cruising-speeds the "2½-Litre" engine—it was really on the order of 2.7 litres in swept volume—was turning only 3100 rpm.

Performance was almost what the works had aimed at. The "2½-Litre" S.S.100 had a maximum officially advertised speed of 98 mph, very close to Lyons's target of 100. Third gear topped out at 75, second at 50, and first gear was good for 27 mph. Through the gears, 60 mph was attainable in about 15 seconds. On the level, starts could be made safely in second gear.

In 1936 and 1937, this was fine performance and enthusiasts who are aware that mechanical brakes—rod-operated Girlings of huge diameter—were used often wonder how this speedy sports car was able to handle an emergency stop. According to the works, these mechanical shoe brakes with Ferodo racing linings would bring the S.S.100 to a standstill from 30 mph in a maximum of 30 feet, a distance at which many modern marvels still juggernaut onward.

The same car bearing an identical S.S.100 Jaguar designation, and weighing the same ready for the road, was available with a larger bore and stroke (82x110 mm.) engine displacing 3485.5 cc. It was introduced late in 1937 for the 1938 season, and was continued in produc-tion until the outbreak of war. With similar dual S.U. carburetors but a heavier 7-bearing counterbalanced crankshaft and a slightly lower 7.2 to 1 compression ratio, the performance-minded driver had at his command 120-125 bhp at 4250 rpm. This engine, also all-new, was the forerunner of the XK engine of 1948. So equipped, the S.S.100 Jaguar sports two-seater was officially known as the "3½-Litre" model. Its maximum speed was theoretically 105 mph with the tachometer reading approximately 4750 rpm. This was peaking over the maximum power point but was within the durability limits of this excellent engine if this speed was not sustained for extended periods. Acceleration to 60 mph was 11.3 seconds, fairly good acceleration today for a comparably powered vehicle using pushrods.

A specially modified 3½-Litre S.S.100 with a 12.5 to 1 compression head gulped equally special fuel, and averaged 118 mph while lapping the Brooklands course in late 1937 with Tommy Wisdom at the wheel. Other off-the-shelf 2½ and 3½-Litre S.S.100 Jaguars won rallys, trials, and races all over the British Isles and on the Continent. In 1936, the first year of full production, a 2½-Litre S.S.100 won the International Vila Real race, the "best performance" award in the Royal Automobile Club Rally and numerous other events. In 1937, the Honorable Brian Lewis and the famed Tommy Wisdom captured the Manufacturers Team Prize in the Royal Automobile Club Rally in S.S.100s. At other races, the victorious Jaguar snarls were heard. Many years after introduction, Ian Appleyard drove a carefully preserved 3½-Litre S.S.100 Jaguar to another best-performance and was awarded a coveted Coupe des Alpes—a special silver cup for driving the Rally route without loss of points—in the 1948 Rally, a backbreaker for even the most up-to-date cars.

Though reflecting elegance, this S.S.100 Jaguar's lines are marred by the bobbed fenders.

(*Jaguar Cars Ltd.*)

Cobbled mudguards and a domestic V-8 engine have demoted this otherwise lovely S.S.100 Jaguar to "special interest" category. *(Author's photo)*

In America, to own an S.S.100 Jaguar in either the
2½ or 3½-Litre version is the ambition of many today.
So eager was one enthusiast that he too hastily bought
one cobbled, on the sly, with a Chevrolet V-8 engine,
much to his chagrin when he learned the facts.

Production of all S.S. Jaguar models grew rapidly to
the rate of more than 12,000 cars a year, a respectable
figure before World War II for cars of prestige and
genuine quality. Most numerous of the S.S. Jaguars were
the saloon and convertible coupe models. Fewer than
800 of the S.S.100s were built in either 2½ or 3½-Litre
versions.

### 2½ Litre S.S. Jaguar Family Cars

The less exciting but more numerous six-cylinder
passenger-type S.S. Jaguars were without formal series
designations or names from late 1935 until the autumn
of 1937. They were simply catalogued as "2½-Litre"
models. The same 2663.7 cc., overhead-valve, 102-bhp
engine that gave the S.S.100 its improved performance
drove through a 4-speed gearbox with altered ratios.
Weighing approximately 3300 pounds at the curb, the
rather heavy "saloon" had a top speed of around 87
mph and could easily cruise all day at 65 mph without
danger to the rugged 7-main-bearing engine while
handling almost like a sports car and delivering around
14-16 miles to the U.S. gallon of gasoline.

The frames were built to Jaguar designs by Rubery
Owen, a specialty firm catering to the needs of the
industry at large. The wheelbase of 119 inches was the

The late 1935–37 S.S. Jaguar saloons are officially 2½-litre models. *(Jaguar Cars Ltd.)*

same as that of the S.S.I which was finally phased out
by the end of 1936. The overall length, however, was
shortened to 178 inches and 180 inches, respectively,
for the four-door, closed cars and the sporty, two-door,
four-seater, open Tourer.

## 4-Cylinder, 4-Door S.S. Jaguar Sedans

The smaller, 4-cylinder S.S.II went out of production
around mid-1936. In its place to accommodate the
4-cylinder market, a four-seater, all-steel-bodied, four-
door saloon was introduced at the same time as was the
2½-Litre line. On a frame developed from the S.S.II,
the wheelbase grew slightly to 108 inches and the length
overall became 170 inches. The carefully crafted body
was also all-steel. The interior was exquisitely finished
with polished hardwood, leather upholstery, and a full
set of instruments.

The effect was a smaller edition of the large series.
The 1608.5 cc. engine was based upon the familiar
Standard Twelve used on some of the S.S.II models in
1934, but with a new Jaguar-designed cast iron cylinder
head with overhead valves. Three main-bearings carried
the counter-balanced crankshaft. Other detail refinements of the engine boosted the output to 65 bhp. A
single S.U. carburetor and a 40 to 60-pound forced-feed
oil system were used. More than 500 pounds heavier
than the S.S.II, the new "1½-Litre" S.S. Jaguar 4-
cylinder sedan had a maximum speed of 70 mph,
delivered over 20 miles to the gallon (U.S.) of low
octane fuel, and could accelerate considerably faster

In 1936, the 1½-litre saloons replaced the S.S.II. (*Jaguar Cars Ltd.*)

than the replaced series with the L-head engine of the same volume. The "faster" acceleration, however good in 1936, would be rather unimpressive today. To reach 60 mph took around 35 seconds.

Few changes were made on the 4-cylinder Jaguar until late in 1937 when the kittens of the Jaguar litter for the 1938-1940 seasons were introduced with a newly engineered engine block bored out to 73 mm. The stroke remained the same 106 mm.—like that of the 6-cylinder power plants—but the larger 1775.8 cc. piston-displacement boosted the taxable (formula) rating to 13 horsepower. Fuel consumption remained about the same but the top speed increased to 76 mph and acceleration by some 30 percent despite the increase in curb weight of a shade over 100 pounds. Curiously the advertised brake horsepower was not changed.

The size of the 1¾-Litre S.S. Jaguar 4-cylinder model was increased, though, to 112.5 and 173 inches for the wheelbase and length overall in that order. The wheel tread, front and rear, was widened to 55 inches allowing the body width to be increased from a narrow 58 to a more sensible 65.5 inches. The wider tread improved stability and handling and the wider body allowed more generous interior dimensions so that three persons could be comfortably seated in the well appointed rear compartment. The former, somewhat skimpily proportioned, four-seater sedan had become a moderately priced, high-quality, five-seater family car with accommodations in keeping with beautiful classic styling. A drop-head five-seater coupe was also available from early 1938 to 1940 on the 4-cylinder chassis.

The pre-war, all-steel-bodied saloons, about 1938–40, included 2½ and 3½-litre models. Car and lady both look better than some modern versions. (*Jaguar Cars Ltd.*)

*Larger 2½ and 3½-Litre Jaguars*

The 2½-Litre S.S. Jaguar range for 1938 through the first few months of the war in 1940 was paired with a new 3½-Litre series and new drop-head coupes. Both 6-cylinder engines, common to the S.S.100 Jaguar sports cars, were available on identical chassis with wheelbases slightly extended to 120 inches because of transmission modifications. Although the length increased by 8 inches, the body width shrank 1 inch. Improvements in the structural design of the body, however, increased the useful width of the rear seat sufficiently to seat three persons rather than two as in the 1936-1937 series.

The two specified engines were the same as those of the S.S.100, as were the transmission gears, but the rear axle gears were altered to give more favorable overall ratios to compensate for the larger, heavier chassis and bodies of the family cars. Known officially as the "2½-Litre" and "3½-Litre" Jaguars, these magnificent cars were duplicated almost exactly in later years as the much sought after post war models of 1945 through 1947.

In the interests of roadability, the front and rear treads were made 2 inches wider, and such characteristics of the S.S.100 as flat cornering, stability and lack of front end sway were duplicated to a remarkable extent in the family cars. Solid front axles, worm steering, semi-elliptic leaf springs and Luvax lever-type, hydraulic shock absorbers were retained all around. In

July, 1939, piston-type, hydraulic shock absorbers were introduced on all 6-cylinder S.S. Jaguars for a more controlled, quiet ride. The performance and quality of these classic-lined S.S. Jaguars rivaled those characteristics in the ultra-high-calibre cars costing two and three times as much—marques like the Alvis, Bentley, Lagonda, and others. The 2½-Litre Saloon or Coupe was still capable of doing around 87 mph while the 3½-Litre version topped out at 90 mph according to the works. In accelerating from a standing start through the gears to 60 mph, the 3½-Litre Saloon reached this comfortable cruising speed in about 15 seconds.

Comfortable cars, the sedans ignored small road irregularities and cushioned the larger chuckholes and bumps with silent efficiency. S.S. Jaguars possessed an excellent firmness vs. softness compromise. The all-steel bodies were welded units comprised of many separate stampings and formed "a complete shell of immense strength." Rubber blocks were used in the body-to-frame mounts. Well soundproofed for the time, the interiors were luxurious, having comfortable armrests, leather over deeply sprung, padded individual front seats and bench type rear seats, and thick carpets on the floors and over the transmission hump. Polished walnut graced the doors beneath the windows, and the facia panels which were fully instrumented. Refinements abounded—even the door hinges were equipped with grease nipples to eliminate annoying squeaks. The spare wheel rested beneath the luggage boot, the door—or lid—of which was hinged horizontally at the bottom. Opened, the boot—or trunk—lid lay flat and contained a set of tools which included a spark plug socket, an extra plug, ignition point gauges, grease gun, an emergency starting crank, and numerous wrenches, pliers, screwdrivers, etc. The frame ends, front and rear, contained jacking lugs.

The graceful vertical grille was capped with a badge marked "S.S. Jaguar." Above and behind the front bumper were dual, high intensity road lamps to supplement the large Lucas headlights. Most of the sedan models were fitted with sliding roof panels as standard equipment. The drop-head convertibles had landeau irons and the tops could be half-folded to the coupe de ville position, or dropped completely into the well behind the rear seat. The tops—"hoods" in England—of the drop-heads were head-lined in the European manner.

At £385, the "2½" and "3½-Litre" multi-seaters were excellent buys. Rare today in America, a well preserved example is worth as much as when new. As for the S.S.100 Jaguars, they are rarer still and command as much as the buyer is willing to spend or—more correctly—to invest.

### The Pre-War S.S.100 Coupe—Forerunner of the XK 120

The mystery car of the pre-war S.S. Jaguar line was the often heard of but seldom seen S.S.100 Coupe, a fixed steel-topped model shown only in 1938 at the London Show. This beautiful car's lines eventually were to see the light of day on the XK 120 Coupe more than a decade later.

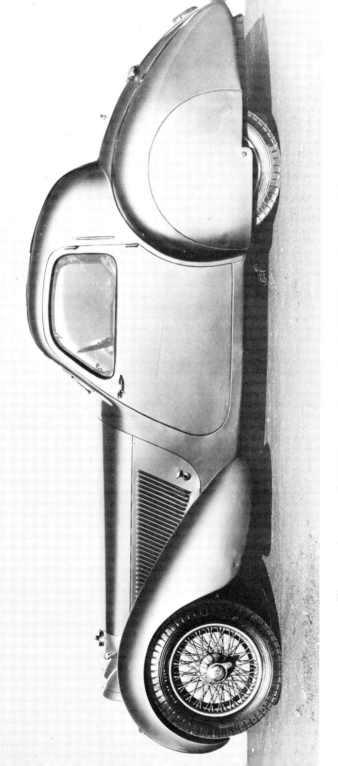

The mysterious, one-off S.S.100 coupe displayed in late 1938 influenced post-war designs.
*(Jaguar Cars Ltd.)*

By mid-1938, S.S. Jaguar Cars Ltd. had come full circle—works chassis were becoming popular as the basis for special bodies by coachmakers in England and on the continent.

During the Battle of Britain, major portions of the Jaguar works were destroyed in the blitz. Coventry, the "Detroit of Britain," was a top priority target of the enemy. The archives suffered too, making a complete photo record of all of the pre-war models very difficult to compile.

Before the war's end in Europe, the name of the firm was changed again, the management wisely deciding that the initials "S.S." should be dispensed with for obvious reasons associated with the Nazi terror. Consequently S.S. Cars Ltd. became Jaguar Cars Ltd. in March, 1945, as the post-war cars and worldwide exports were in the planning stages.

|  | S.S. JAGUAR 1½-Litre 4-seater 1936–37 | S.S. JAGUAR 1½-Litre 5-seater 1938–40* | S.S. JAGUAR 2½-Litre 4-5 seaters 1936–37 | S.S. JAGUAR 2½-Litre 4-seat Tourer 1936–37 |
|---|---|---|---|---|
| Cylinders & Valves | 4 OHV pushrods | 4 OHV pushrods | 6 OHV pushrods | 6 OHV pushrods |
| Bore, Stroke (mm.) | 69.5 x 106 | 73 x 106 | 73 x 106 | 73 x 106 |
| Displacement (c.c.) | 1608.5 | 1775.8 | 2663.7 | 2663.7 |
| Compression ratio | | 6.8 | 7.3 | |
| Carburetors | 1 SU | 1 SU | 2 SU | 2 SU |
| Brake horse-power @ RPM | 65 @ 4000 | 65 @ 4500 | 102 @ 4600 | 102 @ 4600 |
| Gear speeds | 4 | 4 | 4 | 4 |
| Gear ratios | | | | |
| Rear axle ratio | 4.86 | 4.86 | 4.25 | 4.25 |
| Length overall (inches) | 170 | 173 | 178 | 180 |
| Width overall | 58 | 65.5 | 67 | 66 |
| Height overall | 56 | 60 | 58 | 58 (top up) |
| Tires | 18 x 4.75 | 18 x 5.25 | 18 x 5.50 | 18 x 5.50 |
| Wheelbase | 108 | 112.5 | 119 | 119 |
| Tread, front  "     rear | 48 48 | 55 55 | 54 54 | 54 54 |
| Curb weight (approx.) | 2750 | 2900 | 3300 | 3280 |

* Though the engine was 1¾ litres in cubic capacity, the '38–'40 passenger model was officially called the "1½-Litre" by the works.

| | 2½-Litre S.S. 100 1936–40 | 3½-Litre S.S. 100 1936–40 | 2½-Litre 5-seaters 1938–40 | 3½-Litre 5-seaters 1938–40 |
|---|---|---|---|---|
| Cylinders & Valves | 6 OHV pushrods | 6 OHV pushrods | 6 OHV pushrods | 6 OHV pushrods |
| Bore, Stroke (mm.) | 73 x 106 | 82 x 110 | 73 x 106 | 82 x 110 |
| Displacement (c.c.) | 2663.7 | 3485.5 | 2663.7 | 3485.5 |
| Compression ratio | 7.6 | 7.2 | 7.6 | 7.2 |
| Carburetors | 2 SU | 2 SU | 2 SU | 2 SU |
| Brake horse-power @ RPM | 102 @ 4600 | 125 @ 4250 | 102 @ 4600 | 125 @ 4250 |
| Gear speeds | 4 | 4 | 4 | 4 |
| Gear ratios | 1.00  1.37 2.11  3.60 | 1.00  1.21 1.86  3.17 | 1.00  1.37 2.11  3.60 | 1.00  1.21 1.86  3.17 |
| Rear axle ratio | 4.00 | 3.80 | 4.50 | 4.25 |
| Length overall (inches) | 150 for '36–'37 153 for '38–'40 | 150 for '36–'37 153 for '38–'40 | 186 | 186 |
| Width overall | 63 | 66 | 66 | 66 |
| Height overall | 54 (top up) | 54 (top up) | 61 | 61 |
| Tires | 5.25 x 18 | 5.25 x 18 | 5.50 x 18 | 5.50 x 18 |
| Wheelbase | 104 | 104 | 120 | 120 |
| Tread, front    ”    rear | 54 54 | 54 54 | 56 | 56 |
| Curb weight (approx.) | 2600 | 2600 | 3530 | 3530 |

# 3

# *Early Post-War Jaguars—*
# *The Last of the Classics*

WHEN peace came, the works faced the "brave new world" as Jaguar Cars Ltd. Although bustling with new designs and ideas, the engineering department was forced to defer them because of a decision of management.

The demands of a car-starved public had to be satisfied in the quickest, most practical manner. Under Lyons's direct management, Jaguar department heads unanimously agreed that the most sensible course would be to resume production where the war had intervened. Competitive car makers were doing the same, and for Jaguar to do otherwise would be a waste of valuable time. Production, therefore, commenced in July.

Consequently, when the first London Show in six years opened in October, 1945, the cars on the Jaguar stands for the 1946 season were virtual duplicates of the familiar models of 1938-1940. Advances in metallurgy and improved production techniques learned while producing aircraft components and other military equipment during the war, however, assured cars of even better quality despite the retention of pre-war designs. The pre-war engines were largely of Jaguar design, but they had been produced to order by external suppliers. Lyons next decided to manufacture the same engines in the Jaguar works and the facilities for such were quickly prepared between VE Day and July.

The reputation enjoyed by the firm's products was such that the most particular car buyers—and people of taste were the natural Jaguar prospects—cared little that the style and specifications were repeats of the successful pre-war models. Lyons and his staff reasoned that retention of the classic lines would not only attract new buyers but also retain the business of the thousands of satisfied customers, many of whom had become devotees of the Jaguar marque in the pre-war years.

That these considerations were sound was confirmed immediately. Although many Britons were forced to await delivery for as much as two years due to governmental restrictions devised to bolster the war-ravaged economy, the exporting of cars to Europe began almost immediately and was followed, in January, 1947, by shipments to the United States where Max Hoffman of New York City was the first distributor. In those early post-war years, British car makers were required to export at least 70 percent of their output in order to facilitate the earning of foreign exchange upon which Britain depended for economic survival.

By 1947, Jaguar output had risen to a rate of more than 10,000 cars per year. Overseas members of the British Commonwealth imported thousands of Jaguars, and Belgium and Switzerland were other bright spots.

Modifications to satisfy the American market were few: conversion to left-hand drive, the addition of "over-riders" (bumper guards) so necessary for our rough-and-tumble parking, and eventually substitution of turning signal lights for the English "trafficators." The latter, incidentally, offer far superior visibility under any and all conditions.

Though William Lyons and his engineers preferred 6-cylinder engines, the success of the 1938-1940, smaller, 4-cylinder S.S. Jaguar family cars and the anticipated post-war demand for economy, particularly in Europe, resulted in the re-introduction of the 1½-Litre model. Not exported to the U.S.A., more than 12,000 of them were built, with England and the British Commonwealth absorbing most of the output before production stopped in 1949. Virtually unknown in the United States, the little Jaguar was an interesting car.

*The Last 4-Cylinder Jaguar*

The engine was the pre-war, Standard-based but Jaguar-redesigned, overhead valve version. In every respect this car was a small edition of the big models. Having two fewer cylinders, the 1½-Litre Jaguar, as it was officially named, was equipped with a single exhaust system, one S.U. carburetor, and smaller Girling 10⅝-inch-diameter, mechanical brakes. The performance, as one might imagine, was like that of the pre-war model already discussed. Of compact size as the accompanying specifications detail, the structural components, from the rigid box-section frame to the all-steel bodies, were built with the same meticulous attention to the smallest details. The finish was hand-rubbed, engine flywheels and the 4-bearing crankshafts were polished as well as statically and dynamically balanced. The finest cowhide upholstery was sewn over deeply padded, individual front and bench-type rear seats, thick pile carpeting covered the floors, and positive acting, dual, electric windshield wipers were used. (The latter aids to vision in inclement weather had been used on most British cars since the early thirties. American motorists were evidently unaware of such devices until the fifties.)

In common with the senior Jaguars, the 1½-Litre 4-cylinder cars were initially all four-door sedans. The walnut interior trim on the window sills and facia panels retained the relationship to traditional British coachwork. Newly designed instrument dials with white figures on black backgrounds improved night driving comfort and decreased windshield reflections. The high-headlight beam indicator lights were changed from red to blue. Though seemingly small details, such changes added to driving safety and ease at the wheel and were common to all the new Jaguars, large and small.

It is intriguing to wonder about the impact that the 4-cylinder Jaguar might have had upon the American market had it been exported with the same vigor put behind the large models. It is certain that the number of Jaguar users and the number of drivers who love quality first and foremost would have been considerably increased.

## Catalogued But Not Produced

When the first post-war models were catalogued for sale, the Jaguar 100 (formerly the S.S.100) sports car and the one-only similarly designated sports coupe (of around 1938) were included. None of the latter, however, was produced. A number of the S.S.100 Jaguars found their way to the U.S.A. where they contributed greatly to the re-establishment of sports car circuit and road racing, a great motor sport which had been submerged by track racing in the twenties, a misfortune now in danger of being repeated.

For several years, Jaguar production was largely devoted to helping the replenishment of England's dollar reserves via family cars only. This brings us to one of the most desired of cars, the last of the classic Jaguars, a car that is repeatedly called by the wrong name.

## The Jaguar Called "Mark IV"

Strange as this may now sound, there *never* was a Jaguar Mark IV insofar as Jaguar Cars Ltd. is concerned. The mistake naming of the first 6-cylinder post-war model can be laid to several sources: (a) to some zealous dealers anxious to explain the designation of the Mark V which followed; (b) to imported-car enthusiasts for like reasons; (c) to owners who were and are justifiably proud of a prized "Mark IV"; or (d) to program

Mrs. Ruth Hellman's elegant 1948 Jaguar 3½-litre saloon is a frequent concours entry. *(Author's photo)*

A dual-overhead camshaft XK 120 engine has replaced the original OHV engine in this 1948 3½-litre Jaguar saloon. (*Author's photo*)

directors of imported car or classic car shows. In all fairness, automotive writers, too, may very well have contributed to the "Mark IV" confusion.

Quite obviously, American car makers sometimes indulge in the pastime of selecting a combination of letters and numbers on the basis of real or imagined sales appeal. "QED-300" just might have that magic, selling sound. Manufacturers in other countries are no less likely to be influenced by similar temptations.

The designating of automobile models is frequently amazing and confusing. William Lyons's firm, however, has always been comparatively forthright and practical in this regard. The reader—particularly the enthusiast—is invited to reflect upon the absence of a "Mark III" in the history of Jaguar. There was an S.S.I and an S.S.II and it follows that there could have been a Mark III when S.S. cars became Jaguars. The S.S.100 was probably so named to explain the performance potential.

Nevertheless, Lyons insisted upon logical designations and relied upon quality to attract appreciative buyers. There was a definite reason for the curious sequence of Roman numeral "Marks" as will be explained when we come to the Mark VII in a later chapter.

To clarify and record the proper, official name of the Jaguar model in question, the so-called Mark IV was officially catalogued by Jaguar Cars Ltd. as either the "2½-Litre" or the "3½-Litre" model of the 1946 through 1948 seasons depending upon which of the two engines was installed. All were five-seater, four-door sedans until the two-door drop-head convertible, with the same seating arrangement, was revived in 1947. Unlike a few other manufacturers, M.G. and Singer for example, Jaguar never brought back the 4-5 passenger, open-Tourer models.

Despite the near duplication of the 1938-1940 range of cars, the specifications for the 1946-1948 models are given at the end of this chapter. There were a few minor changes to be sure: early in 1947 automatic ignition control replaced the manual spark advance but the convenient manual choke remained as did the dual exhaust system with its advanced ceramic coating. "For Grace, Space, Pace" became the Jaguar slogan. Certainly the "2½-Litre" and "3½-Litre" models had the styling

Although Jaguar Cars Ltd. never designated any model Mark IV, the early post-war 2½-litre and 3½-litre models have come to be so called. (*Author's photo*)

Jaguar cat and graceful radiator grille, large headlights, decorate nose of the models wrongly called Mark IV. (*Author's photo*)

to justify "Grace." The spacious interiors supplied the "Space" and slightly altered transmission ratios and improved spiral-bevel gears in the new hypoid rear axles boosted maximum speeds to about 90 mph for the smaller-engined cars and 95 mph for the larger. Though acceleration was only slightly affected, the performance verified the advertised claim of "Pace" despite a slight decrease in compression ratios.

With semi-elliptic leaf springs all around plus the beam-type front axle, the so-called Mark IV was an intriguing car to Americans who were familiar with technical details. To a generation of drivers weaned on the advertisements extolling "knee action" and sponge-soft front coil springs, the handling, roadability, comfortably controlled ride and accurate steering of the big Jaguar sedan were a revelation. The huge 13½-inch-diameter Girling mechanical brakes—the last such on any Jaguars—were amazingly efficient and so well engineered that even today a properly maintained set are soft and positive in use. The rather slow steering, 4¼ turns lock-to-lock, was quicker than on most American makes. That all American drivers had not become too

Beam type front axle, semi-elliptic leaf springs and mechanical brakes are shown on this much used 1948 Jaguar 3½-litre saloon. (*Author's photo*)

The post-war 3½-litre drop-head coupe was popular in America.

*(Author's photo)*

The luxury of polished wood and soft leather in the 3½-litre drop-head. Note the top is lined. Windshield opened; gear lever was short; steering wheel adjustable. (*Author's photo*)

flabby was evidenced by the way the few thousand imported Jaguar sedans quickly found buyers who apparently decided that the "Mark IV" looked like the fine car it was, with huge headlights, conservatively dignified lines and all. When production of the first post-war, 6-cylinder cars was discontinued in mid-1948 to make room for the first really new model since the war, the overseas Jaguar market was well prepared.

Engine was easy to work on in the so-called Mark IV Jaguar 3½-litre.
(*Author's photo*)

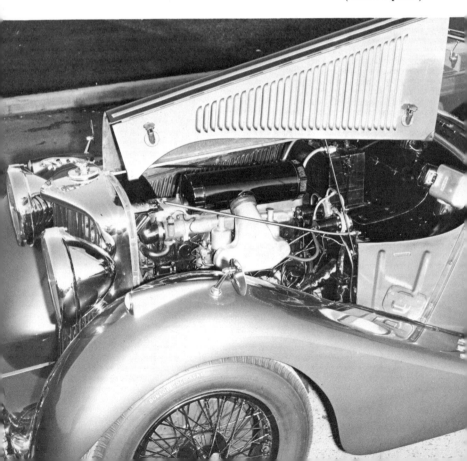

Cloth headliner gave interior of the 3½-litre drop-head coupe the feel of a hardtop. Note pleated upholstery. (*Author's photo*)

### *The Mark V—Traditional Lines Concealed Modern Engineering*

When the Mark V was introduced in September, 1948—a month before the London Show—the tradi-

"For Grace, Space, Pace" was a realistic works appraisal of the popular post-war Jaguar 3½-litre models. (*Author's photo*)

Last of the classic Jaguars was the beautiful Mark V, also the first of Lyons's cars to have hydraulic brakes, torsion bars, and moulded-in headlights. (*Author's photo*)

John Thomas, born in Cornwall, displays the badge of the Duchy on the grille of his Mark V which is still in daily service. (Author's photo)

Rear wheel spats, headlights and heavier bumpers are major exterior changes on Mark V. *(Author's photo)*

George Rauch's drop-head Mark V has captured many concours awards.
(*Author's photo*)

tionally conservative lines had been deftly blended with a touch of modernity. The headlamps were neatly moulded into the fenders and the windshield and door pillars were made slimmer without decreasing the strength of the body structure. Aft of the cowl, the styling was not otherwise changed.

Two body styles were offered, the four-door sedan and the two-door drop-head convertible. Each type comfortably seated five adults in the leather upholstered, walnut-trimmed interiors so typical of fine British cars.

The same two highly successful and extremely durable 6-cylinder engines were available. These had moderate improvements in the ignition timing and fuel system and slightly lower compression ratios. The developed bhp was unchanged but maximum speeds were decreased to 86 and 91 mph, depending on which engine was fitted, due to the newly designed frame which had deeper and heavier longitudinal members. The latter were box-sections as previously and had jacking lugs fitted fore and aft. The new frame and heavier, stronger bumpers added about 200 pounds to the overall weight.

The Mark V was the last Jaguar with camshaft in the block.
(*Author's photo*)

First Jaguar with independent front suspension (wishbones and torsion bars) and hydraulic brakes was the Mark V. Note screened air scoops to brake drums. (*Author's photo*)

Independent front wheel suspension was the most revolutionary chassis change since the marque Jaguar succeeded the S.S. range in 1936. Wishbone members of unequal length and longitudinal torsion bars replaced the beam-type front axle and semi-elliptic front springs. Leaf springs were retained in the rear. The steering— admittedly a bit stiff on the previous model for most drivers—was also improved by a new recirculating ball system. This lessened driver effort. A reduction to 3-1/2 turns, lock to lock, made steering more responsive. The convenient, adjustable steering column, a Burman-Douglas patented device long used by S.S. and Jaguar, was retained. The driver merely loosened the steering column collar and moved the wheel an inch or two to suit himself.

Many Americans found Jaguars satisfying mounts at least partly because of traditional practicalities like

Polished, burled-walnut dashboards and thick carpeting added to Mark V luxury. (*Author's photo*)

separately adjustable front seats, quicker and adjustable steering, and the like.

The Mark V signaled another engineering turning point: Lyons had held out longer than most car manufacturers against hydraulic brakes, but rather than fight the trend any longer, he wisely switched. New 12-inch-

With hood furled to de Ville position, George Rauch's Mark V drophead is a crowd stopper at any Concours d'Elegance. (*Author's photo*)

The Mark V saloon was a spacious family car with comfort and roadability that assured its success in America. (*Author's photo*)

diameter Girling hydraulic brakes were fitted behind the standard disc wheels; wires were optional. Vent openings in the brake backing plates provided air circulation. Late in 1948, the air vents were modified with

Every Mark V carried a complete set of tools in a closed, rattle-free compartment in luggage boot lid. (*Author's photo*)

close mesh screen coverings to prevent the invasion of foreign matter. Some owners, like the author's Cornish friend whose lovely Mark V saloon is shown here, fabricated their own brake vent screens. This particular

As a touring car, Mark V was superb; as a rally competitor, it was a revelation.

(*Author's photo*)

Mark V still handles beautifully and easily despite daily use and long annual trips since it was first registered early in 1949. Enthusiasts, though generally delighted with the much improved Mark V, disliked the cumbersome umbrella type push-and-pull hand brake control fitted to early models beneath the instrument panel. In response to owner reaction, later models were equipped with the more efficient and positive lever-type parking brake that most drivers preferred.

A high-performance family car capable of sustaining exceptionally high cruising speeds for long hours, the Mark V was never intended as a competition machine. Nevertheless, owners with sporting proclivities frequently entered rally and gymkhana events where this large sedan's roadability and fine response enabled it to rack up impressive victories. As an example, Cecil Vard of Ireland took third place in his Mark V in the 1951 Monte Carlo Rally, a grueling event on twisting mountain roads interlaced with high-speed runs.

After nearly 12,000 were built, the Mark V was discontinued in mid-1951 to make way for the all-new Mark VII, the skip in the numerical "Mark" being intentional. The Mark VII, however, was largely a development of the sports car that had electrified the automotive world, the XK 120, whose engine has since sired the powerplants of every Jaguar car, regardless of type to this writing.

| | JAGUAR 2½-Litre Late 1945–48 | JAGUAR 3½-Litre Late 1945–48 | JAGUAR Mark V 2½-Litre Sept. '48– mid '50 | JAGUAR Mark V 3½-Litre Sept. '48– mid '50 |
|---|---|---|---|---|
| Cylinders & Valves | 6 OHV pushrods | 6 OHV pushrods | 6 OHV pushrods | 6 OHV pushrods |
| Bore, Stroke (mm.) | 73 x 106 | 82 x 110 | 73 x 106 | 82 x 110 |
| Displacement (c.c.) | 2663.7 | 3485.5 | 2663.7 | 3485.5 |
| Compression ratio | 7.3 | 6.75 | 7.3 | 7.20 (opt. 6.75) |
| Carburetors | 2 SU | 2 SU | 2 SU | 2 SU |
| Brake horse-power @ RPM | 102 @ 4600 | 125 @ 4250 | 102 @ 4600 | 125 @ 4250 |
| Gear speeds | 4 | 4 | 4 | 4 |
| Gear ratios | 1.00   1.35 1.94   3.38 | 1.00   1.37 1.98   3.37 | 1.00   1.37 1.98   3.38 | 1.00   1.37 1.98   3.38 |
| Rear axle ratio | 4.55 | 4.30 | 4.55 | 4.30 |
| Length overall (inches) | 186 | 186 | 187.5 | 187.5 |
| Width overall | 66 | 66 | 69.5 | 69.5 |
| Height overall | 61 | 61 | 62.5 | 62.5 |
| Tires | 18 x 5.50 | 18 x 5.50 | 16 x 6.70 | 16 x 6.70 |
| Wheelbase | 120 | 120 | 120 | 120 |
| Tread, front ”     rear | 54 56 | 54 56 | 56.5 57.5 | 56.5 57.5 |
| Curb weight (approx.) | 3600 | 3600 | 3840 | 3840 |

NOTE: For 1946 through 1948 model-seasons there was a 4-cylinder car, called the "1½-Litre" model in production; see specifications for the S.S. JAGUAR 1½-Litre model of 1938–1940 at end of Chapter 2. These models were virtually identical.

# 4

# *The Sensational XK Sports Cars*

MOST enthusiasts agree that the M.G. brought sports car fun back to the United States where it had been more or less dormant for nearly twenty years. Granting this, it follows that the XK Jaguars compounded and reaffirmed the exhilerating pleasures of driving fine cars, furthered the enlightment of discriminating motorists, and helped to pierce the foggy aura surrounding Detroit products. Admittedly the XK did not accomplish the revolution among automobile enthusiasts single-handedly. Nevertheless, the XK was the dominant factor insofar as quality and high performance cars are concerned.

Classified as a 1949 model, the first XK 120 roadster went into production late in July of 1948. Publicly introduced late in October at the London Show, the XK 120 roadster was the undisputed star of the show and the hearts of car buffs were easy conquests. To keep the record straight, the closed Coupe was not introduced until March, 1951, at the Geneva, Switzerland, show.

The Coupe was reminiscent of the pre-war S.S. 100 Coupe which was shown in 1938 but not produced.

As time had permitted during the years of war production, Lyons and Heynes had met briefly on occasion to formulate their post-war automobile program. Thus, when peace came to Europe, plans were well along for two basic engines. Four and six cylinder in-line engine layouts won out over considerations of "V" types of eight and twelve cylinders. Lyons and Heynes were both influenced by the great power output of several pre-war, overhead-camshaft, European engines having piston displacements under 4-litres.

Dual overhead camshaft engines had been utilized by only a few limited production British makes between the two great wars. Their more efficient valve systems caused Jaguar management to decide upon such a layout for their new engines. One of Heynes's first moves was to bring Harry Weslake back to Jaguar. Thus it was that the designer of the pre-war S.S. Jaguar pushrod, overhead-valve mechanisms returned to the works during the final year of the war.

The XK engine did not evolve overnight by any means. On the contrary, by mid-1945, a number of experimental designs were under development. All of these carried the X designation. After several 6-cylinder types, along came the XF 4-cylinder test unit with bore and stroke of 66.5 and 98 mm. respectively. The long stroke assured high torque at low speeds, while dual overhead camshafts facilitated high output. On the other hand, the 1360 cc. piston displacement was calculated to achieve fuel economy. This was a virtue in Britain before the war and was again when mass motoring resumed and motorists were faced with higher car purchase and licensing taxes and increased gasoline costs.

Further development enlarged the cylinder bore to assure the power and durability that Jaguar owners would expect. These considerations led to the XJ engine. This 4-cylinder, 1996 cc. (80.5 x 98 mm. bore and stroke) powerplant had an unusually quiet, dual overhead-camshaft layout and a massive, counterbalanced, four-bearing crankshaft. Pre-war experience had proven the virtues of big main bearings. Hemispherical combustion chambers, long favored by several high-performance European makes, permitted more efficiently shaped water jackets for cooling and allowed superior machining, thus improving engine cooling, breathing, and overall efficiency.

One of these XJ Jaguar engines was made available to Lieutenant Colonel "Goldie" Gardner in 1948. Installed in Gardner's astonishingly successful M.G. EX-135 record car, the 2-Litre Jaguar experimental engine developed approximately 145 bhp at around 6000 rpm with special tuning. With this engine Gardner shattered world records both in Europe and on the Bonneville salt flats in Utah.

Lyons, though, had always preferred six cylinders, so a 6-cylinder version of the XJ engine was built with the same stroke but a slightly larger bore of 83 mm. The resulting 3.2 litre engine failed to produce sufficient torque at low rpm's so further experimentation culminated in a new experimental six with the stroke increased to 106 mm. The bore remained at 83 mm. The problem of insufficient torque at low engine speed was solved.

Jaguar management now had two engines with dual overhead camshafts carrying the XK designation—the 4-cylinder 1996 cc. engine with refinements sufficient to upgrade its designation, and a six displacing 3442 cc.

The 3.4-litre six is still available in certain Jaguar models twenty years after the original XK engine design was readied for production. Of course, the current 3.4-litre engine is highly refined. Just how well William Lyons, William Heynes, Harry Weslake and their associates designed this engine is testified to by the retention of the same basic XK features, including dual overhead camshafts, massive 7-bearing crankshaft and all. Higher compression ratios, increased displacement for some models, and refinements galore to be sure, but the engines of all the current Jaguar models are still based upon the XK of late 1948.

The 4-cylinder XK engine was originally scheduled to go into production as a replacement for the pre-war based, overhead valve, 1775.8 cc. engine. However, when the Mark V sedan was introduced for the 1948-49 seasons, Lyons decided to discontinue the smaller sedan, and with it went the 4-cylinder XK.

However, the publicity garnered by the Jaguar 4-cylinder XJ experimental engine in Gardner's M.G. EX-135 record breaker led to expectations by some enthusiasts that Jaguar's long rumored return to sports car production would include a high performance 2-litre roadster to take up where the S.S. 100 left off. This was not to be. It must be remembered that an XK 100 was listed by the works in 1949 and 1950. Never produced, the XK 100 was tested in prototype form and was like the XK 120 in every aspect except for the engine and power train. The potentially great 4-cylinder XK engine, though shelved, provided Jaguar with the results of extensive testing. Subsequent publicity for the new, dual overhead-camshaft layout assured public acceptance of the 6-cylinder version.

The latter point of consideration—public acceptance and satisfaction—is important. Mass-produced cars with overhead camshaft engines had rarely been offered to the motoring public at large. Such engines were not fully understood by most motorists and the average mechanic was hardly more familiar with them. In pre-war years, few manufacturers cared to risk such highly developed machinery on the mass market. The dependability and durability of the XK 120 and improved versions have proven that there is a motor-wise segment of the driving public sufficiently large to warrant basing a sales program upon quality and engineering excellence. The extent of such excellence was particularly amazing in view of a price permitting a purchaser in the United States to get into an XK 120 roadster for a delivered price of around $4,000 anywhere in the country.

*The XK 120*

As they had fifteen years earlier at the advent of the S.S. I, enthusiasts marveled at the obvious elegance and high performance, and the motoring press asked, in effect, "how does Lyons do it?"

A tremendously strong box-section frame was the foundation for the XK's chassis, and the suspension and

Star of the show was the first XK 120 at Britain's first post-war motor show in the Earls Court in October, 1948. (*Jaguar Cars Ltd.*)

A closed coupe was added to the XK 120 line early in 1951.

*(Jaguar Cars Ltd.)*

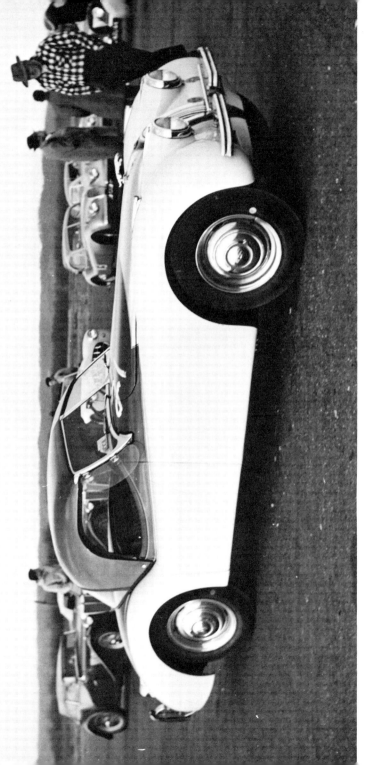

The XK 120 "Chocolate Sundae" tested by the author had a fiberglass top.
(*Author's photo*)

Racing hand-brake, short, remote control gear change lever, bucket seats and a proper panel of instruments made an equally proper impression on Americans. (*Author's photo*)

power train were well contrived to satisfy the most exacting sports car specifications. What met the eyes of enthusiasts, however, upon introduction, was a real eye-opener—something more than they had expected. Instead of the stark body lines and spartan accommodations for driver and passenger that they had been accustomed to, buyers, who would have been elated with the XK engine in the pre-war S.S. 100 Jaguar, found that Lyons's new creation was a smoothly swathed streamlined beauty that was as aerodynamically efficient as it was luxurious and comfortable.

One may surmise that Lyons chose to introduce the Mark V saloon separately in September to test press

The ladies loved the XK 120 and this included the author's wife.
*(Author's photo)*

Irv Goldstine, resplendent in leopard sports jacket, takes his XK 120M to a concours. *(Author's photo)*

This perfectly maintained cockpit is in the Goldstine XK 120M.
(*Author's photo*)

reaction to suspension and brake improvements. More likely, however, Lyons preferred to give the then ultra-modern XK 120 the full benefit of total impact at the Earls Court unveiling in October thus allowing nothing to deflect attention from the long awaited successor to the S.S. 100.

At a Concours d'Elegance most gate-paying visitors come to see fine cars whether or not they understand the technical aspects of a beauty like this XK 120M roadster. (*Author's photo*)

In any event, the XK 120 was an instant success. The long, low hood and adjacent fenders immediately imparted the impression of latent power to Auto Show shoppers the instant they slid behind the steering wheel. Knowledgeable drivers, however, are rarely incurably infected by such a first impression. Once the hood, hinged at the cowl, was lifted, the gleaming 3½-litre, dual overhead-camshaft XK engine provided the necessary bite to overcome almost all reservations.

Some purists sought refuge in cultivated prejudices against the extensive legroom and comfortably soft upholstery afforded by the cockpit. Here was a roadster

An almost dry road despite bitter winter weather permitted 111 mph in author's first test of an XK 120. (*Author's photo by Walt Keuhne*)

The XK 120 introduced dual-overhead camshafts and exceptional performance across the counter to a public nurtured on mediocrity. (*Author's photo*)

sufficiently roomy to allow stowage of the fabric top completely out of sight. The space behind the leather bucket seats was enough for a couple of overnight bags and beneath the rear deck was room for several suitcases. The spare wheel was concealed beneath the floor of the luggage boot and the 16¾-gallon fuel tank (14 British) was larger than on most passenger sedans.

Such creature and touring conveniences were, to some, most non-sporting. To be sure, the works literature plainly stated that an optional 25-gallon gas tank was available for competition-minded buyers, but some enthusiasts remained unconvinced. The XK 120 was just too pretty to be a sports car—it was more like a sporty tourer. Still, the non-glare facia panel, covered with leather to match the upholstery, carried a full complement of Smiths instruments including a tachometer. A manifold pressure gauge at the bottom of the tachometer and an accurate fuel gauge that doubled as a crankcase oil level gauge when a button was depressed were a sufficient tip-off for some that the new Jaguar sports car was as advertised. A warning lamp signaled time to switch to the 2-gallon fuel reserve, too.

Down underneath, the suspension looked familiar only to those who had taken the trouble to examine the Mark V a few weeks earlier. The wheelbase of 102 inches was a shade shorter than its ancestor of 1938, but instead of a rigid front axle on leaf springs, the XK 120 had upper and lower wishbones on each side with longitudinal torsion bars. In the rear, things looked a bit more familiar with very long, silico-manganese, semi-elliptic

Wire wheels alone did not an XK 120M make; these were optional on a stock XK 120 coupe. (*Author's photo*)

leaf springs. Girling telescopic shock absorbers were used and the running gear was properly finished off with 12-inch-diameter Lockheed hydraulic brakes—two leading shoe types—and recirculating ball steering.

Five conventional hub lug bolts secured the optional wire wheels to the XK 120 coupe. (*Author's photo*)

Though luggage boot of XK 120 held limited luggage, it held more than previous sports cars. Spare wheel stowage was a new thing in America. (*Author's photo*)

The turning circle diameter was a handy 31 feet and from lock-to-lock required just 2¾ turns of the Bluemel steering wheel. The wheel was 17 inches in diameter, had a man-sized rim that got away from the clenched-fist

This Jaguar XK 120 was used for everything from racing to hauling a Christmas tree.
(*Author's photo*)

feeling, and was set on the end of a steeply raked column with a long spline and a screw-type collar that permitted about 4 inches of adjustment. This plus about 6 inches of seat adjustment combined to made an efficient and comfortable seat-versus-wheel position for close to the ultimate in driving comfort.

The nearly equal front and rear weight distribution should have convinced the skeptical minority that the XK 120's specifications had been carefully calculated to fill the bill on either track or road. The rear wheels carried about 90 pounds more of the weight than did the front wheels. This happy condition was in marked

The XK 120 engine from the dual S.U. carburetor side.
*(Author's photo)*

contrast to that of most other cars of the period which tended to be nose-heavy though certainly not to the extent that obtains today, especially in American cars. Such a favorable disposition of weight made for light, nearly effortless steering devoid of either under or over-steering despite a total travel weight of at least 3,400 pounds with two persons plus luggage aboard.

Were such a formula followed today in the United States, light and positive steering could be provided, without need of power assist, on family cars up to nearly 4,000 pounds curb weight. Such an engineering course would, however, require courage on the part of manufacturers and a parallel willingness on the part of the public to learn some of the finer points of driving skill. Family cars, even the so-called domestic "sports cars," would then be much safer at any speed.

As enthusiasts were able to examine the XK 120, the critical minority, which initially thought the new sports roadster too good to be true, dwindled rapidly. The word at introduction was that the XK 120 was a 120-mile-per-hour vehicle. This claim plus the comfort refinements on a type supposed to appeal only to rough and ready drivers served, at the outset, to cause some disbelief.

The doubting Thomases did not have long to wait. Before more than a few hundred cars were delivered—all but a scant handful exported to earn urgently needed dollars—Jaguar sent a stock XK 120 to Belgium for high speed tests under the critical eyes and timing instruments of the Royal Belgian Automobile Club. With R.M.V. Sutton at the wheel, a belly pan secured beneath, no windshield, and an optional 3.27 to 1 rear axle, the production roadster handed the automotive world the shock of its life in May of 1949. On the famed Jabbeke highway, a flying mile was run at a sizzling 132.6 miles per hour! Then—to ram home the truth of the manufacturer's claim of true sports car competition performance in an "over the counter production car," the belly pan was removed, the windshield installed, and in full touring gear the same car got off again and covered the same measured and timed mile at 126.45 mph. Both of these amazing runs were made on 74-octane gasoline and in full view of a full corps of British and continental automotive writers. The records of the event further document that Sutton then idled the XK 120 along in front of the press corps at a mere 10 mph in fourth gear without a hint of lugging.

This did it. The XK 120 was unquestionably the production car of the year. Sight-unseen orders came to the works from the four corners of the earth, and Jaguar went on a multi-shift schedule with more than 90 percent of the output devoted to filling the burgeoning export channels. The XK 120 became a waiting-list proposition and nowhere was this more evident than in America.

By late 1949, the XK 120 was the most wanted car in America among the sports car fraternity. Most of the sporting drivers had cut their teeth on the MB-TC. Thus, when the XK 120 came along and offered additional comfort features plus another 40 miles an hour, its acceptance was assured.

*Driving the XK 120*

Not counting several brief periods behind the wheel of an XK 120, the writer's first thorough acquaintance with this marvelous vehicle was when Art Feuerbacher of Clayrich Motors in St. Louis, Missouri, offered his personal roadster for a magazine road test. Because it was winter and bitterly cold, this XK 120 was fitted with a fiberglass hardtop. Sporting a cream and brown special lacquer job, this otherwise stock production car was unofficially dubbed the "Chocolate Sundae."

The "feel" of the XK 120 came in a hurry if one loved cars. Belted into the leather bucket seat, one sat so low he could easily touch the road with the door open. The seat positioned simply as did the adjustable steering wheel and the short gear change lever fell easily to the right hand. Despite sub-zero weather in early mornings, this XK 120 always started at the first touch of the button. Until warm, the chain drive of dual overhead camshafts was audible. With some 40,000 miles on the odometer, the XK 120 purred smoothly after ten minutes or so at which time the camshafts were virtually silent from around 2,000 rpm on up the tachometer.

Speeds in the gears worked out, on this particular car, at 30 mph in first, 61 in second, and 88 mph in third gear. With speedometer error worked out on a measured level mile, the acceleration for a production car in 1952 was sensational. Despite a rather long clutch pedal travel—and the offset pedals took some getting used to —the beautifully synchronized gear box and the convenient shift points made breaking a true 60 mph in a mere 10 seconds dependent only upon quick shifts and smooth clutch work. With practice, the 60 mph mark came down to 9.7 seconds at which point a shift to third and full throttle would take the roadster to a measured quarter-mile in 18 seconds flat. At the quarter-mile, speed was 86 mph.

A quick shift to fourth gear just past the quarter-mile mark at the predetermined true 88 mph—the speedometer was then indicating 93 mph—put one in nearly silent operation except for the sound of the wind whipping the driver's side. The passenger side in that "Chocolate Sundae" XK 120 had a fairly well fitting cloth and plastic window curtain.

The usual problems when engaged in such an enterprise as speed testing were present that winter day despite the selection of a usually deserted road in open country "somewhere" west of St. Louis. However, the road was dry and quite free of snow or ice. Still, with only a few miles of straight road, the car's potential was not quite reached and common sense rather than useless valour under the existing conditions held the maximum attained speed to an indicated 119 mph which, when corrected, computed to 111 mph.

If the XK 120 in its original form had any serious deficiencies, one was the brakes. The 12-inch drums were subject to fade, but they cooled rapidly. At high cruising speeds of 70 or 80 mph, the driver could not help but be impressed with the feeling that there was plenty of power remaining. And there was. The long hood and the wide fenders gave a stimulating view from behind the wheel, which could be adjusted to a perfect location for any physical requirement. At speed, there was a barely perceptible lateral vibration attributable to rather soft springing. On rough roads at low speeds one felt every little irregularity, but this, the writer believes, is as it should be: road conditions should be communicated through suspension and steering to the driver. Once 30 to 40 mph was reached in even the early XK models, the ride smoothed wonderfully.

Taking the curves was a pleasure in an XK 120 roadster, the sharper, the better. Using the gears properly, shifting down if in mountains or just for the fun of it, and then applying accelerator pressure would bring the car through without excessive lean.

One day when stopped at a noisy intersection, another European overhead camshaft car, an expensive marque, which shall remain nameless, pulled up alongside. The camshaft clatter was obvious. The other driver shouted over to the writer that he thought "Jaguars must have some secret about how to keep upstairs camshafts quiet." Such was the way the XK 120 impressed those who knew engines.

There is no reason to doubt the ability of the XK 120 "Sundae" to reach 118-120 mph had conditions been better. Prolonged, slow, heavy-traffic driving produced another problem, a marked tendency to overheat at low speeds. This was corrected by the time the XK 140 came along in 1955 with the cooling system capacity increased to 15 U.S. quarts and the use of a better thermostat. By the time of the advent of the XK 150, the brakes had also been greatly improved.

If the first XK 120 was impressive, the XK 120M (the "M" was for "special equipment") with dual exhausts was even better. Produced during the 1952-54 seasons, most if not all of these were the closed coupe model. Though the XK 120 roadster could, in a pinch as we discovered, accommodate two smallish youngsters behind the bucket seats, the coupe met the small family problem a bit better. Not that the coupe was a "two-plus-two" by any stretch of the imagination, but a couple of children could be toted along for an hour or so seated in the larger luggage compartment behind the seats.

*Driving the XK 120M*

Though mechanically identical to the basic XK 120, the "M special-equipment" model had, as mentioned, a dual exhaust system. One also got wire wheels—though not knock-offs—with this model which delivered initially in the United States for around $4,450 depending upon location. In 1953, further enticement was a price reduction of $500 to $800. A polished walnut instrument panel and full wind-up windows graced this coupe. Not yet, however, had Jaguar come to grips with American traffic and bumper-to-bumper parking. Thus, the bumpers were still of the fragile variety, much to the consternation of owners and insurance companies.

Acceleration of the XK 120M was markedly improved. Though no engine specifications were changed, the rated output increased from the XK 120's 160 brake horsepower at 5200 rpm to 180 bhp at 5500 due to the freer breathing afforded by the dual exhaust system and tuning refinements. The exhaust manifold of a Jaguar has always been a thing of beauty with its ceramic coating and by 1952 this feature was a favorite item of showroom conversation as an easily seen and understood mark of quality. From a standing start, acceleration from first gear into second at 29-30 mph took one to 60 mph in 8.6 seconds. The standing quarter-mile was reached consistently in 16.8 seconds in the XK 120M coupe tested by the writer. Averages of two-way runs through a measured mile produced a corrected top speed of 121 mph with driver only aboard.

For a car weighing a minimum of 3,000 pounds at the curb, and powered with 6 cylinders in-line displacing but 3442 cc., this was the sort of performance that made a Jaguar driver the king of the road. Women loved the Jaguar which handled far easier than even the smallest American convertibles or two-door sedans once street speeds were reached. The single discomforting inconvenience, aside from the offset foot pedals, was the extremely limited visibility to the rear in the roadster version with the top in position. The advent of the coupe corrected this.

*The XK 140*

By the time the new XK 140 was introduced late in 1954 as a 1955 model, more than 12,000 of the XK 120 had been produced, including the M variant, with the majority of them coming into the American market. Although some had feared the complexities of the dual, overhead-camshaft engine, the strange (to American eyes) twin S.U. carburetors and Lucas electric fuel pumps,

The XK 140MC would top 125 mph with comparative ease.
*(Author's photo by Joe E. G. Wherry)*

One had to look closely to identify the XK 140.

(*Jaguar Cars Ltd.*)

A chrome strip on the engine bonnet marked the XK 140 in front. The drop-head model.

*(Jaguar Cars Ltd.)*

The XK 140 drop-head was an all-weather family sports car. *(Author's photo)*

the XK engine quickly racked up an enviable record for durability. The higher-octane, American gasoline decreased the need for the traditional English de-carbonizing, and when owners followed the advice about periodical oil changes and lubrication in the remarkably complete Owner's Manual, it was not at all unusual for the XK engine to perform admirably to 70,000 miles or more without requiring a valve grind. Through the years, reports have been heard that XK engines have far exceeded the 100 thousand mile mark without overhaul or excessive bearing wear.

The XK 140 engine was the same as that of the XK 120M, camshafts and all, with valve head diameters remaining at 1 3/4 and 1 7/16 inches for inlet and exhaust respectively. The output of the XK 140 engine was

Folding top of the XK 140 drop-head stored neatly behind small rear seat. (*Author's photo*)

Polished walnut facias graced the XK 140 drop-head models.
*(Author's photo)*

a rated 190 bhp at 5500 with dual exhausts as standard equipment. From the start of XK 140 production, a "special equipment" model, called the XK 140MC in the States, was optionally available in both roadster and coupe models. Before long a "drop-head" or convertible coupe rounded out the line.

The XK 140MC had, like its XK 120M forerunner, wire rather than disc wheels, and was powered with the 210 horsepower engine of the all-out competition machine, the "C-type," about which more later.

The only styling changes for the XK 140 were a chromed strip down the bonnet, a model change indication for the engine hood, a medallion on the luggage boot lid, and heavier, more rugged bumpers fore and aft to cope with America's parking brutalities. An optional extra on all XK 140 models was overdrive, the excellent dashboard, toggle-operated, Laycock de Normanville unit which functioned on top gear only. Maximum speed was only moderately increased but mileage at highway legal cruising speeds was increased to around 19-20 miles per gallon.

Performance of the production XK 140 was nearly identical to that of the XK 120M. An XK 140MC in good tune, however, told a slightly different story with acceleration through the gears improving slightly to 60

Small children could be accommodated in rear seat of XK 140 coupe.
(*Author's photo*)

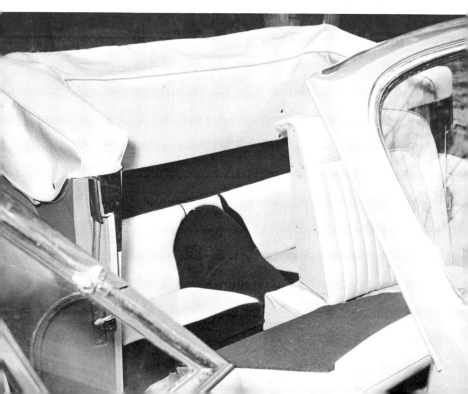

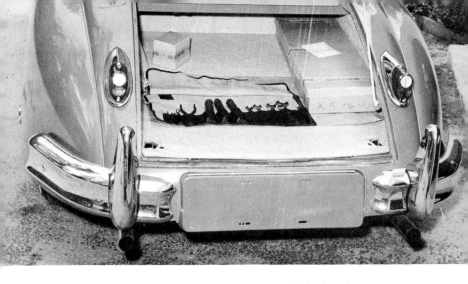

The XK 140 had the heavier bumpers needed in America.
*(Author's photo)*

mph in 8.3 seconds if road surface conditions were perfect. The engine torque, 213 pounds-foot, peaked at 4000 rpm. The transmission of both XK 140 models had closer ratio gears which made for greater flexibility in traffic and better competition performance. Maximum speed was about 126 mph. Law enforcement officers had become extremely sensitive to the XK 120's exhaust rap, so the engineers toned down this noise—music to the ears of enthusiasts—so XK 140 exhausts purred sweetly and rapped only at near maximum speeds.

Steering effort was reduced but remained precise with the adoption of rack and pinion. Handling, if anything, improved with tightened rates for both front torsion bars and rear springs. Driving at low speeds produced slightly increased feel of road bumps, but at highway speeds control was steadier and, thus, comfort was actually improved. For Americans, Borg Warner automatic gear boxes were optional.

The author in the XK 140MC drop-head coupe. *(Author's photo by wife)*

Eugene A. Haunch owns this XK 140 coupe which is used regularly.

(*Author's photo*)

The rear deck of the XK 140 also carried an identifying chrome strip with a special medallion. *(Author's photo)*

*The XK 150*

The queen of the XK sports cars was the XK 150, introduced early in the summer of 1957 in closed coupe and drop-head versions; the roadster returned to the line early in 1958. Major criticism of the previous 120 and 140 models was dissipated for all time—the new XK 150 introduced disc brakes to the world of production cars, the superb Dunlop servo-assisted units that had proven so successful on the "D-type" racing Jaguars covered in the next chapter.

Styling changes were few, amounting to more, however, than on the XK 140 which was phased out of production after only two years. The most noticeable changes in appearance were the one-piece curved windshield and a larger, rounder radiator grille. Not so evident at first glance was the higher body belt line which followed a virtually straight line between the crowns of the front and rear fenders. This was the first major styling change in the original XK lines. Open roadster enthusiasts were let down with this body redesign, but coupe and drop-head buyers praised the change. Even Jaguar couldn't please everybody despite a phenomenally high "batting average."

Through the 1961 season, the standard engines in the XK 150 and the "special equipment" XK 150S model (introduced in 1958) were based on the thoroughly proven 3.4-litre block. For many countries this 3442 cc. engine was available with either an 8.0 or 7.0

Completely new side panels and a one-piece curved windshield gave new lines to the XK 150.
(*Jaguar Cars Ltd.*)

to 1 compression ratio, achieved with relatively low-crown pistons, and milder valving by means of tame camshaft contours. So equipped, the basic XK 150 was rated at 190 bhp at 5500 rpm with a pair of the improved HD.6 S.U. carburetors.

For the American market, however, almost all XK 150 types came in with higher crowned pistons which raised the compression ratio to 9.0 to 1 and the output to 210 bhp at 5500 rpm with 215 pounds-foot torque at 3000 rpm.

Further refinements included a higher valve-lift via camshaft changes, a new cylinder head with straight ports and hemispherical combustion chambers, hotter ignition timing, and a trio of larger HD.8 S.U. carburetors. These raised the output of the 3.4-litre engine to 250 bhp at 5500 rpm. This engine, based on the experience gained with the D and XK-SS types on the racing circuits, was the nucleus of the XK 150S "special equipment" model produced during late 1958 and on into 1961.

In mid-1959, an optional engine with cylinders bored out to 87 mm. for a displacement of 3781 cc. was available in the XK 150S. The compression ratio remained at 9.0 to 1 and the new cylinder head with straight porting was used as were the same three S.U. carburetors. The increased displacement, with everything else remaining substantially the same, was sufficient to raise the bhp to 265 at 6000 rpm while the torque checked out at 240 pounds-foot at 3000 rpm.

The docility and smoothness of the XK 150S engine at low speeds—the most powerful Jaguar up to that time—even in top gear in bumper-to-bumper traffic, was a tribute to sound basic engineering. The seven, huge, crankshaft main bearings, 69.85 mm. in diameter, and the 52.98 mm. connecting rod journals, were the same as in the first XK 120 and would remain so even in the later 4.2 litre models. Such heavy bearings in the "basement" of the engine assured durability. The camshafts in the "attic" were comparably tough. Dynamically balanced and counterbalanced in shops where quality control is practiced, as well as preached, the relatively complex XK engines have been made dependable and calm under all conditions one is likely to encounter on street or track.

Today, nearly a decade after the introduction of the XK 150S, there are precious few new production cars available on the showroom floor for less than $5,000 that can carry two persons in luxurious comfort and turn an honest 130 mph, as a well maintained XK 150S can with either of the two engines. Acceleration with the Laycock de Normanville overdrive locked out was —and still is—little short of terrific: from standstill to a calibrated 60 mph in 7 seconds for either the 3.4 or 3.8 litre version or to 100 mph in approximately 18 seconds. In domestic car talk that's either 210 or 230.6 cubic inches and six rather than eight cylinders for a car weighing a minimum of 3200 pounds at the curb. To compound the evidence of Jaguar mechanical efficiency, any XK in good condition will deliver 16 to 19 miles per gallon of fuel at steady legal highway speeds. Finally, as an eye-opener, examine a typical XK engine in everyday use and it will be most unusual if that engine is not as clean, or cleaner, than an ultra mass-produced model, with a fraction of the mileage, that sold new at a comparable price.

Not that the XK 120 through the XK 150 cars weren't mass-produced; they were, but in the thousands rather than millions. All told, around 34,000 XKs of all types were built between late 1948 and early 1961. More could have been marketed but the care and attention to the slightest details which have always been the guidelines of Sir William Lyons and his associates militated against faster production.

The victories won on the racing circuits on both sides of the Atlantic have been additional testimony to the dual personalities of these great cars. The major victories of Jaguars since 1949 are included with those of the related C, D and type XK-SS at the end of the next chapter.

# SPECIFICATIONS   Chapter 4

|  | XK 120 | XK 120MC | XK 140 | XK 140MC |
|---|---|---|---|---|
|  | Oct. 1948–1954 | (Special Equipment) 1952–1954 | 1955–1957 | (Special Equipment) 1955–1957 |
| Bore, Stroke (mm.) | 83 x 106 | 83 x 106 | 83 x 106 | 83 x 106 |
| Displacement (c.c.) | 3442 | 3442 | 3442 | 3442 |
| Compression ratio | 8.0 7.0 option | 8.0 | 8.0 7.0 option | 8.0 |
| Carburetors | 2 SU H.6 | 2 SU H.6 | 2 SU H.6 | 2 SU H.6 |
| Brake horse-power @ RPM | 160 @ 5200 | 190 @ 5500 | 190 @ 5500 | 210 @ 5750 |
| Gear speeds | 4 | 4 | 4 (overdrive optional) | 4 (overdrive optional) |
| Gear ratios (standard) | 1.00  1.37 1.98  3.38 | 1.00  1.37 1.98  3.38 | 1.00  1.21 1.75  2.98 | 1.00  1.21 1.75  2.98 |
| Rear axle ratios | 3.54 standard 3.77 optional 3.31   " | 3.54 standard 3.77 optional 3.31   " | 3.54 standard 3.31 optional 4.09 overdrive | 3.54 standard 3.31 optional 4.09 overdrive |
| Length overall (inches) | 173 | 173 | 176 | 176 |
| Width overall | 61.5 | 61.5 | 64.5 | 64.5 |
| Height overall | 52.5 | 52.5 | 55.0 | 55.0 |
| Tires | 16 x 6.00 | 16 x 6.00 | 16 x 6.00 | 16 x 6.00 |
| Wheelbase | 102 | 102 | 102 | 102 |
| Tread, front  "   rear | 51 50 | 51 50 | 51.5 51.375 | 51.5 51.375 |
| Curb weight (approx.) | 2950 up | 3000 up | 2950 up | 3025 up |

*Applicable to all models:*

> *Front suspension:* torsion bars and wishbones.
> *Rear suspension:* semi-elliptic leaf springs.
> *Engines:* 6-cylinder in-line with overhead valves actuated by dual overhead camshafts.

# SPECIFICATIONS  Chapter 4  *Continued*

|  | XK 150<br>3.4-Litre<br>1957–1961 | XK 150S<br>3.4-Litre<br>1958–1961 | XK 150S<br>3.8-Litre<br>1959–1961 |
|---|---|---|---|
| Bore, Stroke<br>(mm.) | 83 x 106 | 83 x 106 | 87 x 106 |
| Displacement<br>(c.c.) | 3442 | 3442 | 3781 |
| Compression<br>ratio | 8.0<br>7.0 optional<br>9.0 " | 9.0 | 9.0 |
| Carburetors | 2 SU HD.6 | 3 SU HD.8 | 3 SU HD.8 |
| Brake horse-<br>power @<br>RPM | 190 @ 5500<br>210 @ 5500 | 250 @ 5500<br>(Straight port<br>head) | 265 @ 6000<br>(Straight port<br>head) |
| Gear speeds | 4 | 4 (manual only) | 5 (overdrive only) |
| Gear ratios<br>(standard) | 1.00   1.28<br>1.86   3.38 | 1.00   1.28<br>1.86   3.38 | 0.778   1.00<br>1.283   1.858<br>3.376 |
| Rear axle<br>ratios | 3.54 | 3.54 | 4.09 |
| Length overall<br>(inches) | 177 coupe & d-head<br>176 roadster | 177 coupe & d-head<br>176 roadster | 177 coupe & d-head<br>176 roadster |
| Width overall | 64.5 | 64.5 | 64.5 |
| Height overall | 55 | 55 | 55 |
| Tires | 16 x 6.00 | 16 x 6.00 | 16 x 6.00 |
| Wheelbase | 102 | 102 | 102 |
| Tread, front<br>" rear | 51.625<br>51.625 | 51.625<br>51.625 | 51.625<br>51.625 |
| Curb weight<br>(approx.) | 3150 up | 3200 up | 3200 up |

# 5

## Competition Types C and D
## The Rare XK-SS
## Jaguar Competition Awards

IN 1950 Jaguar organized a works competition department under "Lofty" England's leadership. The XK 120 in the hands of private owners, principally, had been making a name for the marque and it was obvious Jaguars had the power plant upon which to base an all-out campaign to win the major events on the international racing calendar. An innovation for Jaguar, strictly speaking, this official Competitions Department remained active through 1956 by which time the marque's fame as a performance leader was well established.

It was obvious to the management that special cars were needed to challenge the race-bred continental machines being fielded with works support. The most serious rivals were the cars of Sidney Allard, Aston Martin, Alfa-Romeo, Ferrari, Mercedes-Benz, Talbot of France, and the like.

The target selected for assault was that classic event, the annual 24-hour race at Le Mans. Of interest to

Americans particularly, Le Mans was the locale of the first European Grand Prix in 1906 as the result of the thinking of George Gordon Bennett, the American publisher and auto racing buff. Two years later in 1908, the first airplane flight ever made outside the United States began a stone's throw from the famed Dunlop Bridge during the victorious European tour of Wilbur and Orville Wright. To further the background of American interest in Le Mans, the resumption of racing on that circuit in 1921 after World War I saw a Duesenberg driven by Jimmy Murphy win first place. From that date until the last couple of years, Le Mans has proved a stumbling block to all but European contenders.

By 1951, Jaguar was ready to have a go at Le Mans, a twice around the clock grind requiring top acceleration to achieve high speeds on the straightaways, tough gear boxes and superior brakes to handle the sharp turns where suspension weaknesses also become immediately evident, dependable free-revving engines and durable drivers. Jaguar's comfortable driver accommodations also helped, as did better headlights and auxilliary equipment because fair weather cannot be counted on for this June event in France.

The XK Jaguars, in 1950, had two principal drawbacks insofar as full bore competition was concerned. First, the car was comparatively heavier, at a minimum of 3,000 pounds, than its most likely adversaries. Secondly, the drum and shoe brakes were not quite up to the rigors of long distance combat. Illustrating the brake handicap is the experience suffered by John Fitch in an XK 120 at Sebring early in 1951. Fitch and the

Jaguar were doing fine and might well have come in first overall if the brakes had held out. As things developed, though, Fitch had to drive a fair portion of the Six Hour Collier Memorial Trophy Race without brakes. Relying solely on his own skill plus gears and engine braking, Fitch and his XK 120 finished the race and came in first in class. Brakes could have made the XK the overall winner. The 12-inch diameter, shoe-type brakes had too much weight to handle and, thus, were prone to fade under the stress and strain of racing. Even so, the XK cars racked up impressive victories as testified by the table at the conclusion of this chapter.

The works reasoned that Le Mans would be the best gamble because, in the time allotted to prepare cars for the 1951 event, stock production components would have to be relied upon. Such standardization—something of less concern to the potential opposition—does not usually lend itself well to events like the Mille Miglia and Targo Floria. Such events were always prime objectives for makers out to win the Manufacturer's Championship.

## The Type C

With scarcely more than a year of definite preparation, the Jaguar Competition Department fielded a team of three brand new cars. This was the debut of the Type C, sometimes erroneously referred to as the XK 120C.

The confusion in designation is due to the C-type's engine which was a basically stock 3442 cc. unit. The

The 1st place Type C Jaguar in action at Le Mans in 1953.
(*Courtesy of Miles L. Brubacher*)

Old Type C Number 18 in action.
(Photo by Louis Klemantaski, courtesy of Miles L. Brubacher)

Rounding a hard corner, old Number 18, the top money winner in the '53 Le Mans, shows its mettle. (*Jaguar Cars Ltd.*)

Stripped to its tubular steel frame, and displaying three new dual-choke carburetors, this is the famed C-type winner of the '53 Le Mans classic, now owned by Miles Brubacher. (*Courtesy, the owner*)

The entire front end of C-type's body raised to facilitate maintenance.
(*Author's photo*)

principal changes in the engine were high contour
camshafts for improved valve action, a light weight fly-
wheel, a new cylinder head with straight inlet ports and
a special exhaust system. The dual S.U. carburetors were
large, heavy-duty units breathing through a rectangular,

open-front, box-like device which effectively supplied them with an increased amount of cool air. Thus modified, the C-type's XK-based engine developed 210 bhp at 5800 rpm and 220 pounds-foot torque at 4000. (As we have seen, this engine proved so tractable for touring that it was made available later in the XK 140 sports car series.)

A heavy duty clutch was used in conjunction with a works 4-speed transmission. For the 1951 Le Mans race, 3.31 to 1 rear axle gears were used. When the C-type went into limited production for sale to the public, a variety of axle ratios were available with 2.91 to 1 being relatively standard.

The works team of C-types on the Le Mans starting grid in 1951 were driven by Stirling Moss and Jack Fairman, Leslie Johnson and Clemente Biondetti, and P. N. Whitehead teamed with P. D. C. Walker. The mounts of these famous drivers, while not containing the creature comforts of the XK production sports cars, were more conducive to driver comfort over long distances than were some of the hairy opposition. The aerodynamically smooth aluminum body without bumpers and similar touring paraphernalia had side air-outlet louvres to relieve the engine compartment and vents atop the bonnet. The slightest hint of a plexiglass windscreen protected the driver who, for racing, wore helmet and goggles.

The front suspension system was stock XK, wishbones and longitudinal torsion bars with stiffened spring rates. Ultra-quick rack and pinion steering was employed. In the rear, however, a specially fabricated suspension system designed by W. M. Heynes used longitudinal trailing links to position the rear axle. The trailing links in turn were secured to a hefty torsion bar mounted transversely. Stock XK 120 Lockheed 12-inch-diameter, hydraulic, two-leading-shoe brakes were used but with automatic adjustment. Knock-off wire wheels and a smaller-than-stock battery were installed. A 40-gallon (Imperial) fuel tank was beneath the rear deck which contained nothing else. Though C-types were often driven to and from races, no detachable top or luggage space other than nooks and crannies in the cockpit was available.

All of the above was held together by a lightweight tubular frame incorporating side channel members well drilled to decrease weight. Some 800 pounds lighter than the XK 120 roadster, the C-type was also shorter with a wheelbase of just 96 inches.

Jaguar's sudden works-sponsored assault upon Le Mans found the C-types one-two-three in the lead at the end of the first five hours when, suddenly, an oil pressure failure forced Biondetti to retire. Several hours later, during the middle of the night, the car driven by Stirling Moss suffered a broken rod. This left the Walker-Whitehead machine to carry on, which it did, to triumph first overall with a top 2243 miles covered at an average speed, for the 24 hours, of 93.498 miles per hour. Third place on Index of Performance fell to the C-type also. A mighty 4.5-litre Talbot took second place. Yet another honor fell to the Jaguar team: before being forced out, Moss drove the race's fastest lap at 105.2 mph.

Quite naturally William Lyons was delighted and soon released the news that the C-type would go into production. This was the first of a string of victories.

Maximum speed of the Type C Jaguar was well in excess of 140 mph depending upon which of a number of rear axle ratios was fitted for the particular task at hand. Some C-types have been clocked in the neighborhood of 150 mph which is a nice neighborhood for any competition car. As one might reasonably expect, acceleration was tremendous with 6.5 to 7.0 seconds to 60 mph while a standing quarter-mile in 15 seconds was not at all unusual. At a steady 40-50 mph, a gallon of gas would last for 15 miles.

In 1952, misfortune befell the team of C-types at Le Mans. For aerodynamic reasons the radiator grilles had been restyled but they proved too small; all three cars were forced out of the race due to overheating. In 1953, however, C-types were again victorious at Le Mans, and with a vengeance, winning first, second and fourth places.

The one-ton Coventry marvel was a serious threat wherever Grand Prix racing was held. In all, four dozen C-types were built and sold. In the United States they delivered for approximately $5,900. In January, 1953, Dunlop disc brakes were standard. Late in 1953, production ceased. Today a C-type is an eagerly sought collector's item of rare worth; its mechanical features were adopted by the XK 140 "special equipment" models.

## The Type D

When the new Type D Jaguar was introduced in May, 1954, it was a considerably more advanced vehicle

In 1957 Bueb and Flockhart drove this 3.8-litre Type D Jaguar, entered by the *Ecurie Ecosse* of Scotland, to first place overall in Le Mans where it is shown, here, in the S-curves with Ivor Bueb up. (*Jaguar Cars Ltd.*)

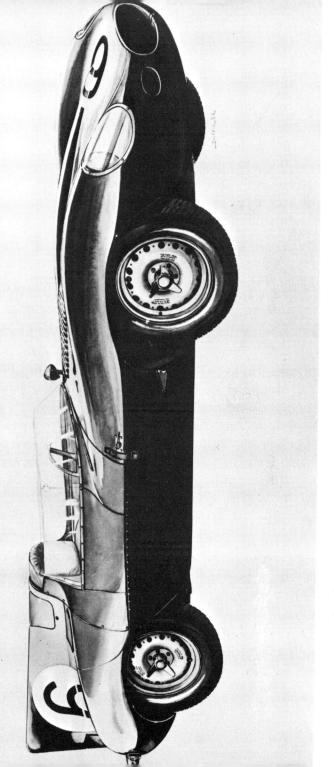

The Type D Jaguar was "the car" on the international racing calendar during the seasons 1954 through 1957, winning the 24-hour Le Mans classic for three straight years. This car proved monocoque construction and disc brakes. (*Jaguar Cars Ltd.*)

than its forerunner. The familiar 3.4-litre engine had a new 9.0 to 1 compression ratio cylinder head with larger intake ports fueled by three dual-choke Weber carburetors. The 250 bhp at 6000 rpm made it the most powerful of any Jaguar engine to date. An external oil tank fed a dry sump via its own oil pump which also supplied lubrication to the dual overhead camshafts.

Entirely new was the monocoque body which, eliminating the conventional frame, was built up of stressed light alloy sheet metal panels around a rigid central section incorporating a front structure. The latter supported the front suspension system, engine and transmission. Front and rear suspensions were refinements of the systems employed so successfully on the C-types. The rear portion of the body was separate and was bolted to the central section. Dunlop disc brakes were used, front and rear, and the C-type rack and pinion steering was retained.

The new D-type looked entirely different; the radiator air scoop was oval in shape and a high aircraft-like fairing extended aft from the driver's side of the cockpit. With an overall length of 150 inches and wheelbase of 90, the D-type was shorter and about 125 pounds lighter than its predecessor.

Tests prior to the Le Mans race indicated that the new D-type's flat out speed was at least 170 mph. Indeed, during the 24-hour event, Stirling Moss was timed once on the straight at 172.8 mph. The 1954 Le Mans was plagued by rain during the hours of darkness. Fuel line and filter stoppages had slowed all three D-types during the last half of the race. Moss overcame this difficulty only to retire with brake trouble while one of the two surviving D-types—the one shared by Ken Wharton and P. N. Whitehead—was forced out after losing all but top gear and developing cylinder head leakage.

Finally, running close to the leading 4.9 Ferrari, Duncan Hamilton brought his D-type (he was teamed with Tony Rolt) in for second place. However, the D-type's second place average speed of 105.0 mph was very close to the Ferrari's average of 105.1 mph. An American Cunningham came in third while a C-type privately entered by Laurent and Swaters heartened the Coventry firm with fourth place.

In 1955, 1956 and 1957, Type-D Jaguars won first places in the Le Mans. Other major international events were similarly dominated by Coventry's star car. What the Jaguar people learned on racing circuits has been passed on to buyers in engineering developments.

The D-type's maximum speed is said to have been around 190 mph in its final 1957-1958 version which had the 3.8-litre engine rated at 265 bhp; a few produced even more power with fuel injection.

*The Dual Purpose XK-SS*

Soon after New Year's Day, 1957, the works let it be known that a new model vaguely termed a "super sports" type would soon become available. The car, later designated XK-SS, was about ready for production when fire broke out in a supply building and spread to a portion of the assembly lines. Around 300 cars were destroyed and a total of around $11 million worth of damage resulted.

The XK-SS was, essentially, a Type D minus tail fin plus full touring equipment. A great fire in the works cut production to a rare sixteen examples. (*Jaguar Cars Ltd.*)

Miraculously, the assembly of the bread and butter sedans and XK 150 models was resumed within a week. When the XK-SS made its belated appearance, it was a touring model of the Type D. A folding fabric top and full windshield, quiet dual exhaust system, side windows and a luggage rack graced the car which, with the road equipment, weighed some 2600 pounds.

Mechanically the XK-SS was almost exactly like the D-type with the 250 horsepower, 3.4-litre engine fitted with triple dual-choke Weber carburetors and all. A 150+ mph sports-competition machine, it would undoubtedly have attracted a large clientele with its superbly comfortable interior and excellent roadability. Unfortunately certain vital parts and tooling being prepared for its production had been destroyed by the fire. Consequently only sixteen were built with deliveries ending early in the autumn of 1957.

*Specials with Jaguar Engines*

During the fifties a galaxy of limited production sports and competition cars were powered by Jaguar engines. These lesser known marques richly deserve a passing mention here as a related aspect of the Jaguar tradition. In random order, these specials were the Lister-Jaguar, the Tojeiro-Jaguar, the H.W.M., the Cooper-Jaguar, the very rare R.G.S. Atalanta, and several others. Some of these cars were built complete to customer orders; a few were sold in kit form. All of them earned varying degrees of fame, mostly in England. In general, these specials were powered with XK engines modified to C and D-type specifications. When they raced, they gave good accounts of themselves, their builders and drivers, and increased the fame of their Jaguar powerplants. Many XK engines were favored for use in high performance boats, too.

## Sir William

The mid-fifties were golden years for Jaguar and the supreme honor for the enterprising Lyons was knighthood conferred by Her Majesty Queen Elizabeth II in 1956 for his outstanding services to his country over a period of years.

Sir William had brought Jaguar to the heights in the sports car world. In the area of family transportation, he was doing the same with sports saloons and limousines that reflected the lessons forged in the heat of racing.

### JAGUAR'S MAJOR RACING AWARDS

#### 1949

*Silverstone* "Daily Express" Meeting, Production Car Race
1st over 3-Litre Class, XK 120 (Moss)
82.19 mph for 1 hr.
2nd over 3-Litre Class, XK 120 (Rolt)

*1950*

*Silverstone* "Daily Express" Meeting, Production Car
Race
>1st over 3-Litre Class, XK 120 (Walker)
>81.88 mph average
>2nd over 3-Litre Class, XK 120 (Rolt)

*Northern Ireland* Tourist Trophy Race, general category
>1st XK 120 (Moss)
>>fastest lap 77.61 mph, winning at 75.15
>>mph
>2nd XK 120 (Whitehead)
>3rd XK 120 (Johnson)
>First place, team prize

*Queensland, Australia,* Road Racing Championship
>1st XK 120, best speed of any production car


*1951*

*Silverstone* "Daily Express" Meeting, over 2-Litre sports
car race
>1st XK 120 (Moss)
>>84.5 mph average
>2nd XK 120 (Dodson)
>3rd XK 120 (Hamilton)
>4th XK 120 (Wicken)
>5th XK 120 (Johnson)
>1st place, team prize

*Northern Ireland* Tourist Trophy Race
          1st Type C (Moss)
                    83.55 mph
          2nd Type C (Walker)
          4th Type C (Johnson, Rolt)
          First three places, over 3-litre class
          Team prize

*Spa, Belgium,* Production Car Race
          1st Unlimited class, fastest lap, XK 120

*Le Mans* 24-Hour Grand Prix d'Endurance
          1st Type C (Whitehead, Walker)
                    average speed 93.498 mph
          Fastest lap, Type C (Moss)
                    105.24 mph

*1952*

*Silverstone* "Daily Express" Meeting
          1st Sports Car Race, Type C (Moss)
                    84.02 mph

*Reims* Sports Car Race
          1st Type C (Moss)
                    98.18 mph
          3rd XK 120 (Scott-Douglas)

*Jersey* Road Race
          1st Type C (Ian Stewart)

*Wakefield* Trophy Race, Ireland
          1st Type C (Ian Stewart)
          3rd XK 120 (Scott-Douglas)

*Prescott & Shelsley Walsh* International Speed Hill
    Climbs
        New Sports Car records, both courses, Type C
        (Walker)

*Spa,* Belgian Sports Car Race
        1st, 2nd, and fastest lap, Type C.

*Hyères, France,* 12-Hour Sports Car Race
        1st Type C (Heurtaux, Crespin)
        Winner, Index of Performance

### 1953

*Reims* 12-Hour Sports Car Race
        1st Type C (Moss, Whitehead)
            105.45 mph
        4th Type C (Sanderson, Scott-Douglas)

*Le Mans* 24-Hour Grand Prix d'Endurance
        1st Type C (Rolt, Hamilton)
            105.84 mph
        2nd Type C (Moss, Walker)
        4th Type C (I. Stewart, Whitehead)
        Distance record, 2539.7 miles

*Nurburgring, Germany,* 1000 Kilometre Race, Over 2-
            litre Production Sports Car Class
        1st Type C (I. Stewart, Salvadori)
        2nd Type C (I. Stewart, Lawrence)
        4th XK 120 (Sanderson, Scott-Douglas)
        5th XK 120 (Keerle, Olieslagers)

*Hyères* 12-Hour Sports Car Race
        1st Type C (Whitehead, Cole)
        2nd Type C (Roboly, Simone)

*1954*

*Reims* 12-Hour Sports Car Race
  1st Type D (Whitehead, Wharton)
   104.47 mph
  2nd Type D (Rolt, Hamilton)
  3rd Type C (Laurent, Swaters)

*Spa* Production Car Race
  1st Type C (Davids)

*Zandvoort, Holland,* Dutch Grand Prix Meeting, Unlimited Class, Sports Car Race
  1st Type C (Sanderson)
  2nd (Scott-Douglas)
  3rd (Laurent)
  4th (van Dieten)
  5th (Thielens)

*Coupe de Paris* Sports Car Race
  1st Type C (Hamilton)

*Sydney,* Australian 24-Hour Sports Car Race, Mount Druitt
  1st XK 120 Coupe (Mrs. Anderson, Swinburn, Pitt)

*Nîmes* International Sports Car Race
  1st Type C (Jonneret)

*Le Mans* 24-Hour Grand Prix d'Endurance
  2nd Type D (Rolt, Hamilton)
  4th Type C (Laurent, Swaters)

*1955*

*Silverstone* "Daily Express" Meeting
> First four places, sports car race over 3-litre,
> Type D (Rolt, Hawthorn, Hamilton,
> Titterington)
> New Sports car lap record (Hawthorn)
> 95.79 mph

*Le Mans* 24-Hour Grand Prix d'Endurance
> 1st Type D (Hawthorn, Bueb)
> 107.07 mph
> 3rd Type D (Claes, Swaters)
> Distance record, 2569.7 miles
> Lap record (Hawthorn)
> 122.39 mph

*Northern Ireland* Tourist Trophy Race
> Lap record, Type D (Hawthorn)
> 94.67 mph

*Sebring* 12-Hour Sports Car Race
> 1st Type D (Hawthorn, Walters)
> Fastest lap (Walters)

*Eire,* Leinster Trophy Sports Car Scratch Race
> 1st Type D (Titterington)

*Northern Ireland* Ulster Trophy Sports Car Handicap
> 1st Type C (Smith)
> 2nd Type D (Titterington)
> Fastest lap and Ulster Trophy (Titterington)

*1956*

*Silverstone* "Daily Express" Meeting, Sports Car Race
Unlimited Class
1st Type D (Berry)
2nd Type D (Brown)
3rd Type D (Flockhart)
4th Type D (Blond)
New lap record, Type D (Hawthorn)
98.48 mph

*Le Mans* 24-Hour Grand Prix d'Endurance
1st Type D (Flockhart, Sanderson)
104.46 mph, 2505.7 miles
4th Type D (Swaters, Rouselle)
6th Type D (Hawthorn, Bueb)
Fastest lap (Hawthorn)
115.83 mph

*Spa* Production Car Race
1st Type D (Sanderson)
Lap record, sports cars Type D (Titterington)

*Reims* 12-Hour Sports Car Race
1-st Type D (Hamilton, Bueb)
111.01 mph, 1332.1 miles
2nd Type D (Hawthorn, Frere)
3rd Type D (Titterington, Fairman)
4th Type D (Flockhart, Sanderson)
Fastest lap (Hamilton)
118.14 mph

*Culton Park* British Empire Trophy Race
        1st  Type  D  (Flockhart)
        2nd  Type  D  (Berry)
        3rd  Type  D  (Sanderson)

### *1957*

*Le Mans* 24-Hour Grand Prix d'Endurance
        1st  Type  D  (Flockhart, Bueb)
            113.55  mph,  2732.4  miles
        2nd  Type  D  (Lawrence, Sanderson)
        3rd  Type  D  (Lucas, "Jean-Marie")
        4th  Type  D  (Frere, Rouselle)
        6th  Type  D  (Hamilton, Gregory)

*St. Etienne, France,* Forez 6-Hour Race
        1st  Type  D  (Flockhart)
        2nd  Type  D  (Lawrence)
        3rd  Type  D  (Hamilton)

# SPECIFICATIONS   Chapter 5

| | C-Type<br>Competition<br>2-seater<br>Intro. 1951 | D-Type<br>Competition<br>2-seater<br>Intro. 1954 | XK SS<br>Super Sports<br>2-seater<br>Intro. 1957 |
|---|---|---|---|
| Bore, Stroke (mm.) | 83 x 106 | 83 x 106 | 83 x 106 |
| Displacement (c.c.) | 3442 | 3442 | 3442 |
| Compression ratio | 8.0 | 9.0 | 9.0 |
| Carburetors | 2 S.U. horizontal | 3 Weber dual choke | 3 Weber dual choke |
| Brake horse-power @ RPM | 210 @ 5800 | 250 @ 6000 | 250 @ 6000 |
| Transmission speeds | 4 | 4 | 4 |
| Gear ratios (standard) | 1.00    1.205<br>1.746    2.979 | 1.00    1.277<br>1.644    2.140 | 1.00    1.286<br>1.657    2.171 |
| Rear axle ratio | 3.31 | 3.54 | 3.50 |
| Length overall (inches) | 157 | 154 | 160 approx. |
| Width overall | 64.5 | 65.38 | 66 approx. |
| Height overall | 38.5 minimum | 44 top of fin | 55 top up |
| Tires | 16 x 6.00 front<br>16 x 6.50 rear | 16 x 6.50 | 16 x 6.50 |
| Wheelbase | 96 | 90 | 90.63 |
| Tread, front<br>"     rear | 51<br>51 | 50<br>48 | 51.5<br>51.5 |
| Curb weight (approx.) | 2175 | 2050 | 2600 up |

*NOTE:* above specification details for these specially conceived cars in their originally introduced form; the variations are covered in the text.

*Engines:* "XK" types; hence all had 6 cylinders, dual overhead camshafts, etc.

*Suspension:* torsion bars front and rear.

*Brakes:* early C-Type drum; later C, all D and SS discs.

# 6

# *The Big Sedans*

WITH the comparative complexities of the dual overhead-camshaft XK engine completely vindicated and with sales of the pushrod-engined Mark V showing no signs of abating, Jaguars repeated their unbroken string of successes in the fall of 1950. When the London Show opened, the Jaguar stand held a completely new family saloon, the Mark VII.

## *Marks VII, VIII and IX*

What happened to Mark VI? There wasn't any. The story is that there was some sort of gentleman's agreement with the Bentley people—and this sounds credible —to eliminate similar designations for models of the two marques. There was a Bentley type 4 but no Jaguar Mark IV, at least not officially. Similarly there was a B 6 Bentley. So the new Jaguar saloon, introduced as a 1951 model, was called the Mark VII.

161

The Jaguar Mark VII introduced the dual-overhead camshaft XK engine to family cars.

(*Jaguar Cars Ltd.*)

Though a comfortable touring car, the Mark VII showed its sporting stance by winning outright the tough Monte Carlo Rally in 1956. (*Jaguar Cars Ltd.*)

Front interior of Mark VII suggested rare blend of sporting and luxury features. (*Author's photo*)

Although a large car by most standards, the somewhat bulbous styling of the body panels made the Mark VII look larger than it really was. By American standards in 1951—or now for that matter—the Mark VII at 196½ inches overall was not overly large but it appeared big.

Mark VII brought British large car luxury to the American mass market.
(*Author's photo*)

The wheelbase of 120 inches did not exceed that of previous Jaguar sedans nor was the wheel tread excessive. Moreover, the width of 73 inches was quite commonplace for family touring cars, especially in America. The customary British restraint regarding front and rear body overhang—the curse of Detroit cars then and now—held the dimensions of the spacious Mark VII within practical limits.

The engine of the Mark VII was the basic 160 horsepower version of the XK engine. The frame was exceptionally strong with pressed steel side and cross members. Profiting from the success enjoyed by the Mark V, the independent front suspension was by wishbones and torsion bars. The rear suspension was also retained—a rigid axle positioned by half-elliptic leaf springs. Contrary to popular talk at the time, the Mark VII was not the sedan version of the XK 120 sports car except for adoption of that type's engine. Actually it was an all-new car based mainly upon the Mark V which it was specifically designed to replace.

Five adults were seated on separate front seats and a bench type rear seat with full-depth foam rubber covered with top quality, hand-sewn cowhide. Folding center armrests increased the comfort in the rear when fewer occupants used the car. Front and rear shoulder widths were 53½ and 57 inches respectively, and legroom exceeded all but large limousines and taxis. The luggage boot was cavernous despite the presence of one vertical-standing spare wheel. The 20 U.S. gallons of fuel were split between two tanks, one in each rear fender.

For the owner who loved to drive, there were a few objections, among them the clumsily extending horn button which intruded itself in tight maneuvers and the slow steering which required 4½ turns from lock-to-lock. The steering, though, was light and exceptionally responsive. Despite its rather long wheelbase, the turning circle diameter was a scant 36 feet. This meant that the big Mark VII could be elbowed into rather constricted parking spaces with more ease than with most modern cars of the same overall length. Without power steering even as an option, the Mark VII was, therefore, superbly engineered.

The public took to the new car immediately wherever the car was sold. Most were exported to America. The roadability was definitely sporting. Despite an all up weight of nearly 4,000 pounds ready for the road, the Mark VII would wind up to a fraction over 100 mph and fairly quickly at that. The four-speed synchromesh gearbox was controlled by a stubby change lever mounted where it belonged, on the floor. From a dead stop to 60 mph took no more than 13 seconds while one could easily zoom, in top gear, from 50 to 70 mph for passing in 10 seconds. The full complement of instruments included a tachometer. The speedometers, incidentally, were unusually accurate. With roadability nearly like that of a sports car, it was a perfect rally car for long, grueling events. In the 1953 Alpine event, one of Europe's roughest on cars and crews alike, the Mark VII chalked up first and third places with second going to a much used Mark V. This achievement brought the Manufacturer's Team Award trophy to Jaguar. (A list of touring car competitions is included in the following chapter.)

In 1953, the 190 bhp XK engine became available. So

Marks VIII and IX offered more power plus optional automatic equipment; styling change was chrome side strip. This is the concours winning Mark IX belonging to Richard Miller. (*Author's photo*)

Mark IX looked larger than it was; but it was still a large car. In good tune, car would clock 120 mph. (*Author's photo*)

Mark VIII and IX models offered dual-tone color schemes. This Mark IX has sunshine roof panel and automatic transmission. (*Author's photo*)

equipped, the big sedan was designated as the Mark VII M. Borg-Warner automatic transmission and dashboard-controlled overdrive became optional as did power steering and brakes.

Other Mark VII developments followed closely and paralleled the regular power increases in the XK engine. Through the Mark VII and Mark IX, styling was stabilized, a factor that undoubtedly added immeasurably to the car's prestige. All told, some 49,000 of the Marks VII, VIII and IX were constructed from

This automatic Mark IX of 1959 was equipped, in Texas, with air conditioning. The small center panel beneath facia contains the "air" controls. (*Author's photo*)

Rear seat occupants in Mark IX had convenient polished wood folding shelves. (*Author's photo*)

late 1950 through 1960. Aside from discreet body trim and dual-tone paint, the design held. No doubt twice or three times this number could have found ready buyers but the ultimate in quality was the Jaguar hallmark and that precluded astronomical production figures.

Disc brakes with servo-assisted action, so outstanding on the racing and sports Jaguars, were fitted to the Mark VIII as an extra cost option; discs were standardized in 1958 on the 3.8-litre, 220 horsepower Mark IX. Only the four-door touring saloon body was built, but with the optional sliding roof panel, small folding tables on the backs of front seats, and hand-rubbed walnut facia

This early Mark IX has a less ornate taillight treatment than the later black saloon.
*(Author's photo)*

panels and window trim, the lack of other body styles was no drawback. When production of the 115 mph Mark IX ceased late in 1961, a new star joined the Jaguar galaxy . . . the Mark X.

*The Mark X*

When the London Show was opened by H. R. H. Princess Alexandra in Earls Court in October, 1961, the Mark X was "such a success it outshone the E-type" in the words of *Australian Motor Sports* magazine half a world away. (The XK-E had been introduced the previous March and was already well launched.)

The new Mark X was completely restyled from bumper to bumper, and was 6 inches longer and 3 inches wider. The hood sloped more sharply to a distinctively redesigned radiator grille, and the rear deck, much longer, concealed luggage capacity to match the largest American family car. Most dramatic of all was the ultra-low roof line representing a decrease of $8\frac{1}{2}$ inches in overall height. Smaller 14-inch wheels facilitated the lower silhouette. The ground clearance alone suffered from the restyling; instead of being the $7\frac{1}{2}$ inches of the Marks VII through IX, it was $6\frac{1}{2}$ inches. The wheelbase was not changed.

More important, really, than the modern lines was the switch to unit-body construction which eliminated the conventional frame. Increasing strength and adding to interior space, the monocoque construction also provided better weather sealing.

There were suspension changes, too—torsion bars

Longer, sleeker lines graced the Mark X, the first Jaguar with dual headlights.

(*Jaguar Cars Ltd.*)

were eliminated in front. Instead, the front wishbones were supported by long coil springs. Independent rear suspension was introduced to Jaguar's big sedans by half-shaft rear axles positioned by a Y-yoke and dual coil springs about midway between the differential and the wheel hubs. Dunlop disc brakes, 10.9 inches in diameter, mounted well inboard in the rear, were standard. Dual master cylinders were used with a brake fluid level warning light on the instrument panel. This made front and rear disc brake operation quite independent of the other, a notable safety factor. Also standard were limited-slip differentials.

Transmissions ran the gamut with four-speed fully synchronized gear boxes being technically standard with either overdrive or 3-speed automatic as optional. As matters developed, most Mark Xs were delivered with the Borg-Warner box.

The engine was the 3.8-litre XK unit tuned to deliver 265 bhp at 5500 and 260 pounds-foot torque at 4000 rpm. Despite a curb weight of right on 4,000 pounds—light for so roomy a car due to the unit-body structure—the performance was sensational with only 10.8 seconds elapsing between zero and 60 mph. A standing quarter mile required a fraction under 18.0 seconds and this performance was with the automatic gearbox. Straight manual 4-speed transmission would have brought these times down to a flat 10.0 and 17.0 seconds with ease. The writer, however, must confess to never having seen a stick shift Mark X; no doubt some were made but few reached the United States. Maximum speed was approximately 120 mph, and there have been reports of slightly more.

The worthy successor to the previous big sedans, the Mark X was, in fact, smaller than the so-called "small three"—the standard-size Chevrolet, Ford or Plymouth models.

Few other family cars such as this were available at the under-$7000 price tag, the approximate level at ports-of-entry.

Handling was improved with less leaning on hard corners, and the faster ratio steering, assisted by power, increased maneuverability. The front tread was wider than previously but the new, tighter, front suspension did increase the turning circle diameter to 37 feet, still from 3 to 8 feet less than other cars of similar size.

For 1964, the Mark X was given the Type E treatment with the change to the 4.2-litre engine but the output remained at 265 bhp. The torque of the 4235 cc. engine increased, however, with the displacement boost and higher efficiency camshafts, to 283 pounds-foot at 4000 rpm. The torque increase—and torque is always more important than horsepower—shaved acceleration time to 8.0 seconds from zero to 60 mph with automatic transmission. With the overdrive gearbox, the maximum speed potential was raised to nearly 125 mph, corrected.

*The Current 420G*

In the autumn of 1966, the same basic car was re-designated the 420G model. Clearly the name refers to the 4.2-litre engine which is continued without changes in specification. Body changes are minor. On the interior, safety padding is used full width above the

The London Show in the autumn of 1966 introduced the new 420G saloon. Principal changes over Mark X were interior. (*Jaguar Cars Ltd.*)

The present Jaguar works in Browns Lane, Coventry, covers one million square feet.

*(Jaguar Cars Ltd.)*

polished wood facia and the clock is now centered in this padding. The front seat mountings have been strengthened, and interior trim is enriched. On the outside, a thin chrome strip runs full length along each side of the body which remains otherwise unchanged. The grille has been altered a little with heavier metal. Overall exterior dimensions remain the same. Shoulder space in front is 57½ inches and in the rear 66½. With bench type seats standard in both front and rear, the 420G is a full six-passenger car of quality and luxury. The central console in the front compartment—as in the 3.8 and 4.2-litre Mark X—limits the middle seating location to children.

Though having superb roadability, and with sporting performance, the Jaguar 420G is a touring car in the grand tradition. Rally and sedan racing competition is the province of the compact sports sedans, the long line which was born in 1955.

# SPECIFICATIONS   Chapter 6

|  | Mark VII | Mark VIIM | Mark VIII | Mark IX |
|---|---|---|---|---|
|  | 1951 thru 1954 | 1954 thru 1955 | 1956 thru 1957 | 1958 thru 1961 |
| Bore, Stroke (mm.) | 83 x 106 | 83 x 106 | 83 x 106 | 87 x 106 |
| Displacement (cc.) | 3442 | 3442 | 3442 | 3781 |
| Compression ratio | 8.0 7.0 option | 8.0 7.0 option | 8.0 7.0 option | 9.0 8.0 option 7.0  ” |
| Carburetors | 2 S.U. H.6 | 2 S.U. H.6 | 2 S.U. HD.6 | 2 S.U. HD.6 |
| Brake horse-power @ RPM | 160 @ 5200 | 190 @ 5500 | 190 @ 5500 | 220 @ 5500 |
| Transmissions | 4 sp. Manual 4 + O'drive | 4 sp. Manual 4 + O'drive 3 sp. Auto. | 4 sp. Manual 4 + O'drive 3 sp. Auto. | 4 sp. Manual 4 + O'drive 3 sp. Auto. |
| Length overall (inches) | 196.5 | 196.5 | 196.5 | 196.5 |
| Width overall | 73 | 73 | 73 | 73 |
| Height overall | 63 | 63 | 63 | 63 |
| Tires | 16 x 6.70 | 16 x 6.70 | 16 x 6.70 | 16 x 6.70 |
| Wheelbase | 120 | 120 | 120 | 120 |
| Tread, front ”    rear | 56.5 58 | 56.5 58 | 56.5 58 | 56.5 58 |
| Curb weight (approx.) | 3950 up | 3950 up | 3950 up | 3950 up |

|  | Mark X 3.8-Litre 1961 thru 1964 | Mark X 4.2-Litre 1964 thru 1966 | 420G 4.2-Litre 1966— |
|---|---|---|---|
| Bore, Stroke (mm.) | 87 x 106 | 92.07 x 106 | 92.07 x 106 |
| Displacement (cc.) | 3781 | 4235 | 4235 |
| Compression ratio | 9.0<br>8.0 option<br>7.0      ″ | 9.0<br>8.0 option<br>7.0      ″ | 9.0 |
| Carburetors | 3 S.U. HD.8 | 3 S.U. HD.8 | 3 S.U. HD.8 |
| Brake horse-power @ RPM | 265 @ 5500 | 265 @ 5400 | 265 @ 5400 |
| Transmissions | 4 sp. Manual<br>4+ Overdrive<br>3 sp. Automatic | 3 sp. Automatic | 3 sp. Automatic |
| Length overall (inches) | 202 | 202 | 202 |
| Width overall | 76 | 76.3 | 76.3 |
| Height overall | 54.5 | 54.5 | 54.5 |
| Tires | 14 x 7.50 | 14 x 7.50 | 14 x 7.50 |
| Wheelbase | 120 | 120 | 120 |
| Tread, front<br>″      rear | 58<br>58 | 58<br>58 | 58<br>58 |
| Curb weight (approx.) | 4050 up | 4050 up | 4050 up |

# 7

# The Sports Sedans and Touring Car Competition Awards

IN the autumn of 1955 the works introduced a new close-coupled five-seater sedan which was, in reality, a family sized version of the XK sports cars. The new sports sedan was received with public and press acclaim at its debut in the London Show in October. Its name was the 2.4-Litre Jaguar.

Despite rumors preceding the introduction, the new 2.4 Litre did not have a 4-cylinder engine. Instead, to obtain fuel economy and reduce prices, an XK dual overhead camshaft 6-cylinder engine destroked to 76.5 mm. was used. The bore remained at 83 mm.; the resulting displacement was 2484 cc. The same durable seven bearing crankshaft was used. The most visible engine alteration was a brace of 24 mm. Solex downdraft carburetors in place of the familiar S.U.s. The optional 7.0 to 1 compression ratio engine used 23 mm. chokes. A 4-speed transmission driving off a single-plate clutch and a low ratio 4.27 to 1 rear axle transmitted the 112 horsepower at 5750 rpm to the rear wheels.

Torque was 140 pounds-foot at 2000 rpm. Once again the XK engine had displayed its remarkable adaptability to modifications while retaining its original toughness and flexibility.

The overall length, 180¾ inches, and wheelbase of just over 107 inches placed the 2.4-Litre model squarely in the compact class. In addition, this model marked the change to integral or unit body-and-frame construction of Jaguar design but built to order by the Pressed Steel Body Company. The four-door sedan's styling was an adaptation of the XK coupe models with a wider but still oval grille but without a hint, however, of fender breaks on the side panels. The weight, ready for the road, was almost the same as that of the two-seaters despite slightly larger overall dimensions and additional passenger accommodations. The 2.4-Litre had Jaguar's first curved, one-piece windshield.

Departing from suspension practice established with the Mark V and XK 120, the new sports sedan dispensed with torsion bars. Instead, coil springs were used in front while the rear axle was positioned by trailing links and half-elliptic springs. Thick rubber blocks were used between the body and suspension members and undercoating further minimized the road noises generally associated with unitized bodies. Servo-assisted Lockheed drum-and-shoe brakes were used all around. The parking brake was of the fly-off, lever-actuated racing type.

The interior of the new model, an "economy" job in comparison to the big sedans, was pure Jaguar with leather upholstered individual front seats and a bench in the rear with a folding central armrest. Hand-rubbed walnut veneer facia and window surrounds maintained the feel of luxury along with high quality, deep pile carpeting. For those with high performance in mind, the Laycock de Normanville overdrive unit was optional. In another two years, Borg Warner 3-speed automatic gearboxes were added to the option list. Instrumentation was complete with the exception of the Smiths tachometer, noticeable by its absence from the facia.

The performance of the 2.4 was exceptional for an engine with 151.5 cubic inches. With the 8.0 to 1 compression ratio head, a maximum speed of 95 mph was attained. Acceleration to 60 mph through the gears took some 16 seconds.

Quickly grabbed up by Englishmen for rally and touring car racing where it achieved immediate success, the 2.4 did not, however, meet with overwhelming popularity in the United States where horsepower, cubic inches and top speeds (with nowhere to use them) were conversational status symbols.

Consequently, late in 1956, the appropriately named 3.4-Litre Jaguar saloon appeared with the 210 bhp, 3442 cc. engine. The larger engine developed, as in the XK 150 and big Mark VIII, a cool 210 pounds-foot torque at 3500 rpm. The new sports sedan had a tachometer with performance to make the revolution counter worthwhile. From standstill to 60 mph took only 9.6 and the quarter-mile mark just 18.0 seconds flat with speed, at the latter mark, 76 mph. Gear speeds were 35 mph in first, 62 mph in second, and 80-82 mph in third. The Smiths speedometer was almost invariably accurate within 6 percent and maximum true speed, with optional overdrive, was 118-121 mph in production tune. This made the 3.4-Litre Jaguar sedan a family work car during the week and a top racing mount for touring car events in off time as the list of victories concluding this chapter testifies. The 3.4 hit the mark, too, in the United States.

*The Mark II*

For the 1960 season Jaguar made a host of improvements in the sports sedan and the new 2.4 and 3.4-litre models were designated Mark II. Dunlop discs, front and rear, were standard equipment along with dual master cylinders and a brake fluid warning light on the instrument panel. The rear tread was increased more than 3 inches and spring rates were recalibrated for vastly decreased rear-end sway, previously troublesome despite the Panhard-type, anti-sway bar. In the front suspension, geometry was altered to raise the roll center.

There were body improvements as well. The rear window was enlarged to full width and windshield pillars were made considerably narrower without decreasing strength. The turn signal lights were lowered and the grille was given a heavier central, vertical bar. The interior was also improved, particularly in front, where a new central console contained heater controls and the radio, the latter an optional item. A tachometer was standard on all Mark II models and, with the matching-size speedometer, was relocated in front of the driver. (The middle location of instruments had been effected to facilitate export to left-hand drive countries.)

The 3.4-Litre Mark II of 1957 was the much improved successor to the 2.4-Litre sports sedan of '55. (*Jaguar Cars Ltd.*)

Mr. and Mrs. Saul Miller own this bright red, concours winning 3.8-Litre Mark II sports sedan. (*Author's photo*)

Engine choices in the Mark II range were increased to three with the 2.4-litre unit being retained and given increased power by means of a new head with hemispherical combustion chambers and improved porting. The 120 bhp at 5750 rpm didn't change maximum speed noticeably but acceleration was increased. The 3.4-litre engine was unchanged. There was no need to revise a good thing, and for buyers who placed a premium on really fierce performance, the 3.8-litre engine, used in the XK 150 and larger Mark IX, was offered.

The suspension and brake changes now enabled the Mark II driver to indulge in genuine sports-type driving, for the 220 bhp of the 3.8-litre compact delivered

The 3.8-litre XK engine fills the engine compartment of the sports sedans. (*Author's photo*)

Six years old and used daily, Saul Miller's 3.8-litre is immaculate. Note the interior: full leather, folding armrest in rear and retractable shelves on backs of front seats. (*Author's photo*)

tremendous performance. (Some 3.8 models were privately modified with the straight port cylinder head mounting three S.U. HD.8 carburetors. So boosted to 250 bhp, the 3.8-litre specials could top 140 mph.) Limited-slip rear axles were also made standard on Mark II 3.8-litre sedans. Equipped with the optional overdrive on top of the 4-speed gearbox, the 3.8 Mark II, with torque of 240 pounds-foot at 2900 rpm on tap, turned in maximum speeds, running light, on the order of 125 mph with acceleration to a true 60 mph in 8.1 to 8.6 seconds. Standing quarter-mile times decreased fractionally to 17.5 seconds. The 3.8 Mark II swiftly carved its own niche as something of a sports car with plenty of space for the children and a generous amount of luggage.

Even as this book is written, the entire Mark II range, including the 2.4-litre version, is still in production. Interestingly, Sir William pulled another of his surprises at the Earls Court show in London in October, 1966, by introducing an economy 2.4 model for the home market, the principal change being synthetic rather than leather upholstery. Scoring "the year's most

The flares and other emergency equipment have been added to this 3.8-Litre Mark II. (*Author's photo*)

Styling of the sports sedans is clearly from that of the XK sports cars. *(Author's photo)*

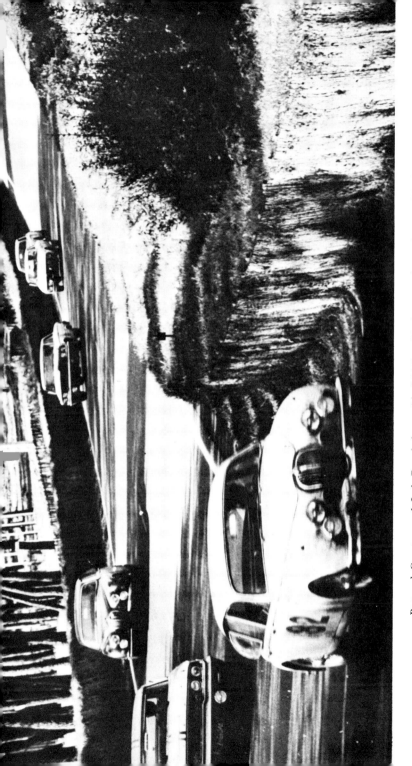

Bernard Cousten and Jack Renel drove this 3.8-Litre Mark II to victory in the 1963 *Tour de France*. Here the car is leading the pack over the Le Mans portion of the nine-day event. (*Jaguar Cars Ltd.*)

The 3.8-Litre Mark II sedan has triumphed in many long distance races. Here Peter Lindner bends the car around a sharp corner during the 1963 Nurburgring Six-Hour Touring Car Race to win the race for Jaguar's third straight victory in that event. (*Jaguar Cars Ltd.*)

dramatic price reduction," in the words of the London *Daily Express,* the latest 2.4 delivers in the United Kingdom for about £147 less than the leather-seated model. It is doubtful, however, whether the lower priced 2.4 will be exported to the U.S.A. where conditions and customer preferences for more power would work against it.

## The Type S

Precisely why Sir William did not wait until the London Show to introduce the elegant Type S has never

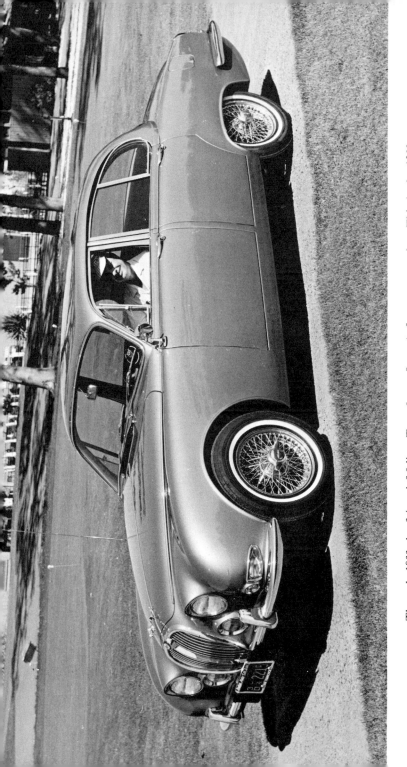

Through 1966 the 3.4 and 3.8-litre Type S was Jaguar's finest sports sedan. This is the 1966 3.8-litre model. (*Photo by Joe E. G. Wherry*)

The Type-S featured longer body, hence more luggage capacity.

*(Author's photo)*

The 3.8-litre Type-S sports sedan.

(Author's photo)

For family touring or motor sports, the S-type had few peers. *(Author's photo)*

Luxury for up to five persons—the 1966 Type S Jaguar.

(*Author's photo*)

Large luggage boot in the Type S carried the spare wheel beneath floor. (*Author's photo*)

been clarified. Suffice it to say that when it was unveiled in September of 1963, it not only caused "a lot of rethinking among the manufacturers of luxury vehicles" as *Autosport* put it, but also caused a lot of drivers on both sides of the Atlantic to do the same.

Built around either the 3.4 or 3.8-litre XK engines, the new S-type was a natural development of the Mark II, complementing it rather than replacing it. Using most components of the Mark II body shell, the S-type's styling resembled it except for the rear deck line which was redesigned along the lines of the big Mark X. Thus, the overall length—not the wheelbase—was extended approximately 7 inches. A completely new, fully independent rear suspension, following generally the transverse links and half-axle shafts of the Mark X,

The instructional "Undo" on the knock-off hub cap of the Type-S still baffles some Americans. (*Author's photo*)

The author bends the S-type hard around a corner during tests.

*(Photo by Joe E. G. Wherry)*

allowed the luggage boot capacity to be increased by one-third. The resulting 19 cubic feet made the trunk one of the largest in the compact car field. The swing axle also enabled the engineers to move the rear seat aft a bit, increasing legroom slightly. The front suspension and disc brake system was like that of the Mark II.

The writer ran a 3.8-Litre Type S extensively. Equipped with automatic gearbox, as are most Jaguar sedans imported into the U.S.A., performance was considerably less than the 121-122 mph maximum with the manual overdrive unit. Top speed with the automatic S-type was 114 mph with zero to 60 mph being 11.4 seconds. The two fuel tanks, one in each rear fender, hold a total of 17 gallons (U.S.) which, even at high cruising speeds, will allow 250-mile leaps between refills if one can resist the temptation to stand on the accelerator when passing or starting.

Though weighing a good 300 pounds more than the Mark II, performance is only slightly decreased. Roadability of the Mark II was excellent; on the S-type it was superior. Passenger comfort in cold weather was assured by a large-capacity heating system with separate controls and outlets for front and rear seats. Drivers accustomed to power steering on domestic cars would find the Jaguar system—shared across the board in such optionally equipped models—unusually responsive. This five to six-seater turned in the unusually small area described by a 33.5 foot diameter circle. A torsional device incorporated in the steering column decreased tendency to wander. Fast $3\frac{1}{4}$ turns lock-to-lock and excellent feel of the road enhanced driving ease and pleasure.

With the manual plus overdrive gearbox, the 3.8-Litre Type S delivered 18 miles per gallon at legal road speeds. Passing acceleration, in top gear, moved the car from a true 60 to 80 mph in 8.5 seconds. This performance was sensational for a 6-cylinder family car of 3600 pounds with just 230.6 cubic inches of engine, the sort of performance requiring another two cylinders plus at least another 100 cubic inches in domestic cars.

### *Types 420 and 340*

For the October 1966 London Show the latest version of the sports sedan, designated as Type 420, was displayed. The engine is the 4.2-litre version as used in the Mark X. The interior now has full-width padding above one of the finest polished wood dashboards available anywhere at any price. An improved Type S, the 420 has dual headlights, a grille like the larger Mark X, and power steering as standard equipment. With disc brakes all around and the 4-speed manual gearbox and overdrive—with the stick on the floor—the price delivered on the East Coast is a very competitive $5,786, the same price asked through 1966 for the 3.8-Litre Type S. Specifications other than the engine are not changed.

For buyers with less expensive tastes, the 3.4-Litre Mark II is now redesignated as the Type 340 sports sedan and delivers for about $4500 with manual transmission.

The newest Jaguar sports sedan is the magnificent Type 420, a development of the Type S with new grille and other improvements, shown here beneath the walls of an ancient castle. (*Jaguar Cars Ltd.*)

Fully padded dashboard and clock in the center are in the new Type 420. (*Jaguar Cars Ltd.*)

As others have asked, how does Lyons offer so much quality and performance at such prices? The method seems to be logical, progressive development without risking untried experiments in the marketplace.

A new grille and dual headlights distinguish the front of the latest sports sedan, the Type 420 with 4.2-litre engine. (*Jaguar Cars Ltd.*)

## RACING AWARDS IN TOURING CAR CLASSES

### 1952

*Silverstone* "Daily Express" Meeting, Touring Car
Race:
1st Mark VII (Moss)
75.41 mph
4th Mark VII (Bradnack)
Fastest lap (Moss)
76.36 mph

### 1953

*Silverstone* "Daily Express" Meeting, Touring Car
Race:
1st Mark VII (Moss)
74.42 mph
Fastest lap (Moss)
76.36 mph

### 1954

*Silverstone* "Daily Express" Meeting, Touring Car
Race:
1st Mark VII (Appleyard)
75.55 mph
2nd Mark VII (Rolt)
3rd Mark VII (Moss)
5th Mark VII (Adams)
Fastest lap (Rolt, Appleyard)
77.48 mph

*1955*

*Silverstone* "Daily Express" Meeting, Touring Car
        Race:
      1st Mark VII (Hawthorn)
        78.92 mph
      2nd Mark VII (I. Stewart)
      3rd Mark VII (Titterington)
      Fastest lap (Hawthorn)
        81.06 mph

*1956*

*Silverstone* "Daily Express" Meeting, Touring Car
        Race:
      1st Mark VII (Bueb)
        80.01 mph
      3rd 2.4 (Hamilton)
      4th Mark VII (Frere)
      New Touring Car lap record, Mark VII
        (Bueb) 81.68 mph

*Spa* Production Car Race, Belgium
      1st touring car class 2.4 (Frere)

*1957*

*Silverstone* "Daily Express" Meeting, Touring Car
        Race:
      1st 3.4 (Hawthorn)
        82.19 mph
      2nd 3.4 (Hamilton)
      3rd 3.4 (Bueb)
      Lap record, 3.4 (Hawthorn, Scott-Brown)
        84.30 mph

*1958*

*Silverstone* "Daily Express" Meeting, Touring Car
Race:
1st 3.4 (Hawthorn)
84.22 mph
2nd 3.4 (Sopwith)
3rd 3.4 (Flockhart)
Record average and record lap (Hawthorn)
87.08 mph

*Silverstone* Grand Prix Meeting, Touring Car Race:
1st 3.4 (Hansgen)
83.92 mph
2nd 3.4 (Baillie)
3rd 3.4 (Crawley)
4th 3.4 (Uren)
Fastest lap, 3.4 (Sopwith)
86.09 mph

*Goodwood,* Whit Monday, Touring Car Class:
1st 3.4 (Hamilton)
78.95
2nd 3.4 (Sopwith)
3rd 3.4 (Baillie)

*Crystal Palace* Meeting, Touring Car Class:
1st 3.4 (Sopwith)
66.88

*Brands Hatch,* August Bank Holiday, Touring Car
Class:
1st 3.4 (Sopwith)
62.5

*Brands Hatch International,* Touring Car Class:
    1st  3.4  (Sopwith)
        63.8

### 1959

*Goodwood* Easter Meeting, Touring Car Race:
    1st  3.4  (Bueb)
        78.4
    2nd  3.4  (Salvadori)
    3rd  3.4  (Baillie)

*Aintree* International, Touring Car Race:
    1st  3.4  (Bueb)
        74.99
    2nd  3.4  (Salvadori)
    3rd  3.4  (Baillie)

*Silverstone* International Trophy, Touring Car Race:
    1st  3.4  (Bueb)
        86.57
    2nd  3.4  (Salvadori)
    3rd  3.4  (Baillie)

*Brands Hatch,* August Bank Holiday, Touring Car
        Race:
    1st  3.4  (Baillie)
     63.41  mph

*Oulton Park* International Gold Cup, Closed Car Race:
    1st  3.4  (Salvadori)
        75.5  mph
    2nd  XK  140  (Protheroe)

*1960*

*Silverstone* "Daily Express" Trophy, Touring Car
        Race:
        1st 3.8 Mark II (Salvadori)
            87.55 mph
        2nd 3.8 Mark II (Moss)
        3rd 3.8 Mark II (Hill)

*Silverstone* Grand Prix Meeting, Touring Car Race:
        1st 3.8 Mark II (Chapman)
            86.5 mph
        2nd 3.8 Mark II (Sears)
        3rd 3.8 Mark II (Baillie)

*Brands Hatch* International, Touring Car Race:
        1st 3.8 Mark II (Sears)
            74.05 mph
        2nd 3.4 (Powell)
        3rd 3.4 (Aston)

*British Empire* Trophy Meeting, Touring Car Race:
        1st 3.8 Mark II (Baillie)
            84.2 mph
        2nd 3.8 Mark II (Taylor)

*Sebring*, U.S. Grand Prix Meeting, Touring Car Race:
        1st 3.8 Mark II (Hansgen)
        2nd 3.8 Mark II (Pabst)

*1961*

RACING AWARDS—ALL 3.8 MARK II CARS WITH OVERDRIVE TRANSMISSION

*Snetterton,* International Race Meeting, Touring Car Races:

> 1st (Baillie)
> 2nd Peter Berry Racing Ltd. (Surtees)
> 3rd Peter Berry Racing Ltd. (Taylor)

*Goodwood,* International Race Meeting, Touring Car Race:

> 1st Equipe Endeavour (Parker)
> 2nd Equipe Endeavour (Hill)
> 3rd Peter Berry Racing Ltd. (Taylor)

*Aintree* International '200' Meeting, Touring Car Race:

> 1st John Coombs Racing Organization (Salvadori)
> 2nd Equipe Endeavour (Sears)
> 3rd Peter Berry Racing Ltd. (McLaren)

*Silverstone* International Trophy Meeting, Touring Car Race:

> 1st Equipe Endeavour (Hill)
> 2nd Equipe Endeavour (Parks)
> 3rd Peter Berry Racing Ltd. (McLaren)

*1961*

*Silverstone* International Race Meeting, Touring Car Race:

> 1st Equipe Endeavour (Parks)
> 2nd Equipe Endeavour (Hill)

*Brands Hatch,* International Race Meeting, Touring Car Race:

    1st Equipe Endeavour (Parks)
    2nd John Coombs Racing Organization (Salvadori)
    3rd Equipe Endeavour (Sears)

*Oulton Park,* International Race Meeting, Touring Car Race:

    1st John Coombs Racing Organization (Salvadori)
    2nd Equipe Endeavour (Hill)
    3rd Peter Berry Racing Ltd. (McLaren)

### Since 1961

All Major British Touring Car Races up to May, 1963, 1st places.

1962 and 1963, Motor 6-Hour *Brands Hatch,* 1st place.

## RALLY AWARDS IN TOURING CAR CLASSES

### 1952

*Dutch Tulip* Rally

    1st in unlimited closed class, Mark VII (Appleyard)

### 1953

*Monte Carlo* Rally, Manufacturer's Team Award:

    Mark VII (Appleyard, Mrs. Appleyard)
    Mark V (Vard, Jolley)
    Mark VII (Bennett, Mrs. Bennett)

*Royal Automobile Club* Rally of Great Britain, over
2.6-litre saloon class:
1st Mark VII (Scott)
3rd Mark VII (Warwick)

*Dutch Tulip* Rally, Saloon Class:
1st Mark VII (Appleyard, Mrs. Appleyard)
2nd Mark VII (Mattock, Christian)

*Rallye du Soleil,* Over 2-Litre Class Touring Cars:
1st Mark VII (Thirion)

*1954*

*Monte Carlo* Rally
Best performance on the road section, Mark
VII (Adams, Titterington)
2nd & 3rd, in over 1½-litre class (Adams,
Titterington, Vard, Jolley)
Two highest placed cars in rally.

*Dutch Tulip* Rally, over 2.6-litre Normal Series Production Car class:
1st Mark VII (Boardman, Duckworth)

*1955*

*Monte Carlo* Rally
Winner of Charles Faroux Challenge Trophy,
for highest placed manufacturer's team,
all Mark VII (Adams, Vard, Appleyard)

*Royal Automobile Club* Rally of Great Britain, Over
2.6-Litre Grand Touring Class:
1st Mark VII (Stross, Pointing)
2nd Mark VII (Tyrer, Kemp)

*Dutch Tulip* Rally, 2.5 to 3.5 Standard Touring Class:
> 1st  Mark VII (Boardman, Whitworth)
> 2nd Mark VII (Cooper, Edge, Cranshaw)

### 1956

*Monte Carlo* Rally
> 1st Mark VII (Adams, Bigger)

*Royal Automobile Club* Rally of Great Britain, over
2-litre Production Touring Class:
> 1st 2.4 (Bleakley, Hall)

### 1957

*Mobilgas Round-Australia* Reliability Trial, over 2.5-
litre class:
> 1st Mark VIII (Mrs. Anderson)
> > Probably toughest event of type in world,
> > covering around 10,000 miles

*Great American Mountain* Rally
> 1st 2.4.

### 1958

*Royal Automobile Club* Rally of Great Britain
> > 1st Normal & Improved Series Production
> > class, 2-2.6 litres: 2.4 (Waddilove)
> > 1st Normal & Improved Series Production
> > class, over 2.6 litres: 3.4 (Brinkman)
> > 2nd Normal & Improved Series Production
> > class, over 2.6 litres: 3.4 (Sopwith)
> > 3rd Normal & Improved Series Production
> > class, over 2.6 litres: Mark VII (Rowe)

*Dutch Tulip* Rally
> 1st, 2-2.6-Litre Normal Series Touring Car Class: 2.4 (Morley)
>
> 2nd over 2.6-Litre Normal Series Touring Car Class: 3.4 (Brinkman)

*R.S.A.C. Scottish* Rally
> 1st over 2.6-Litre Touring Class: 3.4 (Parkes)

### 1959

*Monte Carlo* Rally
> Charles Faroux Challenge Trophy awarded to best nominated team won by three Jaguars (Parkes, Walton, Brinkman)

*Dutch Tulip* Rally
> 1st 3.4 (D.J. Morley, G.E. Morley, Hercock)

*Tour de France*
> 1st Touring Class: 3.4 (Ramos, Estager)

### 1960

*Lyon Charbonnieres* Rally
> 1st Touring Car Class 4: 3.4 (Gentilini, Justamond)

*Dutch Tulip* Rally
> 1st Grand Touring Car Class 3-4 Litres: 3.4 (Haddon, Vivian)
>
> 1st Normal Series Touring Cars 2.5-4 Litres: 3.8 (Parkes, Howarth)
>
> 1st Improved Series Touring Cars, 1.6-4 Litres: 3.8 (Boardman, Whitworth)

*Greek Acropolis* Rally
>    1st Touring Class over 2,500 cc.: 3.8
>        (Von Westerholt, Kuehling)

*Alpine* Rally
>    Alpine Cups awarded to: 3.8 (Behra, Richard)
>        and 3.8 (Parkes, Howarth)
>    1st Touring Category, over 2000 cc.: 3.8
>        (Behra, Richard)

*Royal Automobile Club* International Rally
>    1st Touring Car Category, over 2500 cc.: 3.8
>        (Berry, Sears)

*1961*

*Circuit of Ireland* Rally
>    Class 4, over 1600 cc. class: 1st, 3.8 Mark II
>        (Parkes, Howarth)
>    Class 6, over 1300 cc. class: 1st, 3.4
>        (O'Connor, Rorke, Cuff)

*Tour de France,* Touring Car Category:
>    1st 3.8 Mark II (Consten, Renel)
>    2nd 3.8 Mark II (Jopp, Baillie)
>    3rd 3.8 Mark II (Duboit, Ertager)
>    4th 3.8 Mark II (Orsine, de Maria)
>    1st, 2nd, and 3rd in all the 8 Hill Climbs and
>        6 Circuit Races of this event.
>    1st and 2nd in special test in Corsica.

|  | 2.4-Litre 1956 thru 1960 | 3.4-Litre 1957 thru 1960 | 2.4 Mark II 1959— | 3.4 Mark II 1959— |
|---|---|---|---|---|
| Bore, Stroke (mm.) | 83 x 76.5 | 83 x 106 | 83 x 76.5 | 83 x 106 |
| Displacement (cc.) | 2484 | 3442 | 2484 | 3442 |
| Compression ratio | 8.0 7.0 option | 8.0 7.0 option | 8.0 7.0 option | 8.0 7.0 option |
| Carburetors | 2 Solex | 2 S.U. HD.6 | 2 Solex | 2 S.U. HD.6 |
| Brake horse-power @ RPM | 112 @ 5750 | 210 @ 5500 | 120 @ 5750 | 210 @ 5500 |
| Transmissions | 4 sp. Manual 4+ O'drive 3 sp. Auto. | Same | Same | Same |
| Rear axle ratio | 4.27 Manual 4.55 O'drive 4.27 Auto. | 3.54 Manual 3.77 O'drive 3.54 Auto. | 4.27 Manual 4.55 O'drive 4.27 Auto. | 3.54 Manual 3.77 O'drive 3.54 Auto. |
| Length overall (inches) | 180.75 | Same | Same | Same |
| Width overall | 66.75 | Same | Same | Same |
| Height overall | 57.5 | Same | Same | Same |
| Tires | 15 x 6.40 | Same | Same | Same |
| Wheelbase | 107.33 | Same | Same | Same |
| Tread, front  "     rear | 54.63* 50.13 | 54.63* 50.13 | 55.0 53.33 | 55.0 53.33 |
| Curb weight (approx.) | 3100 up | 3200 up | 3250 up | 3300 up |

* Tread, front only, 1 inch wider with disc brakes.

| | 3.8 Mark II 1959— | 3.4 Type-S 1964— | 3.8 Type-S 1964— | 420 1967— |
|---|---|---|---|---|
| Bore, Stroke (mm.) | 87 x 106 | 83 x 106 | 87 x 106 | 92 x 106 |
| Displacement (cc.) | 3781 | 3442 | 3781 | 4235 |
| Compression ratio | 8.0 | 9.0 8.0  option 7.0    " | 9.0 8.0  option 7.0    " | 9.0 |
| Carburetors | 2 S.U. HD.6 | 2 S.U. HD.6 | 2 S.U. HD.6 | 2 S.U. HD.6 |
| Brake horse-power @ RPM | 220 @ 5500 | 210 @ 5500 | 220 @ 5500 | 255 @ 5500 |
| Transmissions | 4 sp. Manual 4 + O'drive 3 sp. Auto. | Same | Same | Same |
| Rear axle ratio | 3.54 Manual 3.77 O'drive 3.54 Auto. | 3.77 Manual 2.93 O'drive 3.77 Auto. | 3.77 Manual 2.93 O'drive 3.77 Auto. | 3.77 Manual 2.93 O'drive 3.31 Auto. |
| Length overall (inches) | 180.75 | 187.8 | Same | Same |
| Width overall | 66.75 | Same | Same | Same |
| Height overall | 57.5 | 54.5 | Same | Same |
| Tires | 15 x 6.40 | Same | Same | Same |
| Wheelbase | 107.33 | Same | Same | Same |
| Tread, front "    rear | 55.0 53.33 | Same | Same | 55.25 54.25 |
| Curb weight (approx.) | 3300 up | 3600 up | 3600 up | 3600 up |

# 8

# The XK-E for Sports and Two-Plus-Two Grand Touring

WHEN the XK-SS sports car was cut short by the fire in the works in 1957, the outlook for an across-the-counter 150 mph Jaguar was dimmed. The XK 150 upheld the tradition of fast Jaguar sports cars although falling a bit short in performance in the view of some enthusiasts. Rumors kept alive the expectation that Lyons would pull another surprise—possibly even re-enter international grand prix racing from which the firm withdrew in 1956.

Sir William's surprise was introduced March, 1961, in Switzerland when the Jaguar stand in the Geneva Show literally glittered with sleek two-seater roadsters and closed coupes. The XK-E had arrived and the power-plant was the D-based 3.8-litre dual overhead-camshaft engine mounting the high efficiency cylinder head and three heavy duty S.U. carburetors. With 265 bhp and 260 pounds-foot torque at 4000 rpm, this was a car! The total effect was a combination of the best features of the competition Type D and its road version, the XK-SS,

221

The XK-E closed two-seater was first shown in Geneva, Switzerland, in March, 1961.
(*Jaguar Cars Ltd.*)

plus a host of new features. The motoring press and enthusiasts went wild over the XK's successor.

The new model was not entirely unexpected; Briggs Cunningham had entered a mysterious, streamlined car in the 1960 Le Mans race. The 1960 Le Mans car had independent rear suspension and looked as though the body contours had been born in a wind tunnel. The independent rear suspension of the new XK-E was most

In an E-type Graham Hill leads a Ferrari through the Woodcote corner at Silverstone in 1963 during the Fifteenth International Trophy Meeting. (*Jaguar Cars Ltd.*)

The 3.8-Litre XK-E roadster was also introduced in 1961. *(Author's photo)*

Three large S.U. carburetors help develop 250 horsepower in the mighty, race-bred XK-E. *(Author's photo)*

welcome although the new model was in the grand tourismo rather than the grand prix tradition. The five years since the factory had last raced had been well spent on the packaging which was to give the public a 150 mph road car with the XK engine as its nucleus.

Preceding the big Mark X sedan by a half-year, the XK-E played a major role in re-introducing four wheel, independent suspension on British cars. The XK-E also introduced aerodynamic body design to the Jaguar

As capable on track as on the street, the XK-E roadster's cockpit is comfortable and efficient with a proper stick shift. (*Author's photo*)

range with a new unit-body chassis based upon the experience already gained with the compact mass-produced sports sedans. The packaging was in three integrated assemblies of rigid, shaped, 20-gauge sheet steel forming a unit of immense strength.

The foundation of the body was the floor pan and box section longitudinal members, on each outside extremity, forming the sills. The propeller shaft tunnel provided additional resistance to stress as did U-shaped cross-members. A tubular and box-section subframe forward of the firewall held the front suspension, steering mechanism and engine. The rear body component was composed of the luggage boot floor, the rearmost body bulkhead and a separate sub-frame. The latter carried the final drive assembly.

Whereas the sports sedans had forsaken torsion bars in the front suspension, the new Type-E retained the long bars as on the XK 120 through 150 models. An anti-roll bar was fitted transversely to the lower wishbones.

The rear suspension, however, is all new and is successfully retained on the latest XK-E types. Lower, transverse tubular members are secured by pivots at the differential case and wheel carrier on each side. Half-shaft axles, with universal joints at the differential, carry the rear wheels and function as the upper transverse members of the rear suspension assembly. The differential is of the limited-slip type using multiple-plate clutches to eliminate wheel spin as when one wheel is on a slippery surface. The torque is, thus, automatically delivered to whichever rear wheel is on solid ground. Double coil springs, each surrounding a telescopic shock absorber, are employed. Radius arms between the lower transverse links and the body position the rear swing axle longitudinally. The differential cage is secured in rubber mountings to the sub-assembly which, in turn, is bolted to the body structure.

The brake system works through dual master cylinders to 12-inch-diameter Dunlop disc brakes which are self-adjusting. Mounted at the wheel hubs in front and inboard beside the differential in the rear, the brakes are servo-assisted. (The latest S-types and the new Type 420 sports sedans employ an almost identical rear suspension.) These brakes are superb, virtually impossible to fade, and, with the limited-slip differential and excellent suspension, give the XK-E grand sports cars the near ultimate in roadability for cars in their class.

The interior is all grand tourismo with a short gear change lever on the floor, a full battery of instruments directly in front of the driver set in a non-glare panel, padding across the facia-top, and racing-type steering wheel with a wood rim. Adjustable two ways, for reach and height, the wheel gives positive steering through rack and pinion in just 2¾ turns lock-to-lock without need of power. Highly maneuverable, a 180-degree turn requires only 37 feet between curbs. Two bucket seats and luggage space behind the seats provided ample space for two only. The open two-seater came, in standard form, with a folding top which stored neatly. An option was an easily attached fiberglass hard top which could be installed without removing the folded roadster top. The wide curved windshield was fitted with three electric wipers; all around visibility was excellent.

Around 500-600 pounds lighter than the XK 150, the XK-E had the performance the enthusiasts had hoped for. Maximum speed with the roadster's top stowed away was from 146 to 149 mph. The coupe was 2.3 mph faster due to decreased wind resistance. The acceleration was fierce with 60 mph reached in 6.5 seconds, and the standing quarter-mile in from 14.5 to 14.8 seconds. Fuel consumption at legal sustained highway speeds could always be counted upon to reach around 18 miles per gallon. The fuel tank held 17 gallons (U.S.). The red line on the tachometer was at 6000 rpm and the gear speeds using 5500 rpm as shift point, were 43 mph in first, 75-79 in second, 110-115 in third, and 146-152 mph in fourth depending upon whether the mount was the roadster or closed coupe. For such performance the XK-E came fitted with Dunlop RSS tires and the works suggested pressures of 40 p.s.i. front and rear. The higher 3.31 to 1 rear axle ratio was also necessary for such performance.

In 1964, the XK engine with bore increased to 92.07 mm. became available and the car was designated as the 4.2 XK-E. The rated horsepower was not raised but the torque was boosted to 283 pounds-foot at 4000 rpm. The maximum speed was thus increased 2 or 3 mph and acceleration fractionally. The same two body styles were available and are still at this writing.

## The XK-E Two-Plus-Two

The 1965 season saw the XK-E's popularity supreme in its class when it delivered, in the U.S.A., at $5600 up. Clearly, however, there was a need for a more spacious interior. One-car families with a yen for the XK-E were

The XK-E "Two-Plus-Two" is a family sports car par excellence.

*(Author's photo)*

Low, sleek, long; the XK-E four-seater.

*(Author's photo)*

Engine bonnet of the XK-E, when forward, discloses front wishbone and torsion bar suspension on the off-side of the 4.2-litre engine. (*Author's photo*)

unable to find space for the youngsters. So late in 1965 the "Two-Plus-Two" was introduced (with the 4.2 litre

engine) as the solution to the problem. Again Jaguar
scored an instant success.

Naturally a bit more length was required. The resulting body structure changes produced an overall length
of 184.5 inches on a wheelbase of 105 inches. The additional 9 inches of length provided the necessary space for
a bench seat behind the bucket seats, both of which
folded forward for access through doors which were
wider. About 2 inches higher to gain interior space, the
Two-Plus-Two actually looks lower. Nearly 400 pounds
were added to the all-up weight—a small matter, really,
as the curb weight is still only about 3000 pounds.

The 4.3-litre, triple carburetor engine develops 265 bhp in the current
E-type "Two-Plus-Two." (*Author's photo*)

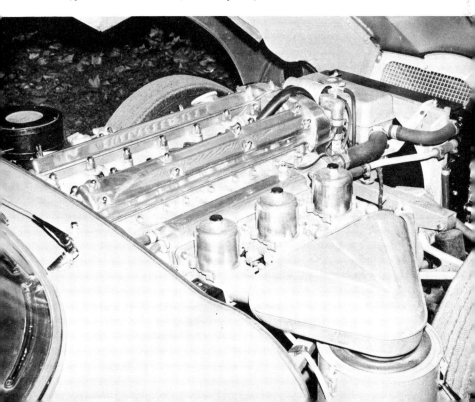

The front interior of the 4.2-litre E-Type closed four-seater. Note the short lever on the automatic gearbox quadrant. (*Author's photo*)

Because many customers outside enthusiast ranks were being attracted to Jaguars, the works made the dual-range Borg-Warner automatic gearbox optional with the control lever on the central console. The four-speed, all-synchromesh transmission is still standard. Owing to the family nature of the Two-Plus-Two, the standard rear axle ratio is 3.54 to 1 which brings the top speed to about 130 mph which should be sufficiently rapid. For those whose blood flows faster, quicker rear axle gears are available through Jaguar dealers who are everywhere.

Most XK-E Two-Plus-Two Jaguars come into the United States with the automatic transmission and 3.31

to 1 rear axle gears. Thus equipped, the sleek, green
Two-Plus-Two tested by the author delivered a true
60 mph in 8.7 seconds the first few runs. The automatic
gearbox would not be this writer's choice. Repeated
runs eventually brought the zero to 60 mph time down
to an average of 8.4 seconds. As the car showed only

A bit more wheelbase permits comfortable rear seating in the XK-E
"Two-Plus-Two." (*Author's photo*)

There's remarkable luggage space beneath the rear deck of the E-type.
(*Author's photo*)

some 3,000 miles on the odometer, it is reasonable to expect that more thorough running-in would bring acceleration to 60 mph close to the flat 8 second mark. With the manual gearbox, 7.5 seconds should be attained without difficulty.

In traffic, the family XK-E is docile at the lowest speeds, and quiet, too. The dual exhausts release only the most pleasant low octave burble of sound—a purr to be more exact.

Adults, preferably not six-footers, find the "occasional" rear seat quite comfortable for an hour or two. Children, though, can be very comfortable and family accommodations were the aim. When two are touring, additional luggage space is available by moving the backrest of the rear seat forward, thus extending stowage space considerably. As in the short-wheelbase two-seaters, the spare wheel is secured in a rattle-free mount

All car, the XK-E "Two-Plus-Two."

(Author's photo)

A four-seater that can be tuned for 150 mph, the Jaguar XK-E.

*(Author's photo)*

below the floor of the luggage space where the spare, in turn, secures a unique set of hand tools. The finest in genuine leather and carpeting is hand-fitted throughout the two and four-seater models and this adds to comfort and sound-deadening as well. At $6500 up delivered in the U.S.A., there is little competition for the Two-Plus-Two.

Does the XK-E race? Yes, in the two-seater, 96-inch wheelbase versions. In 1963, three E-type coupes triumphed over a sparkling field to win first, second and third places at Silverstone during the Grand Touring car event in the Fifteenth International Trophy races. The E-types are regularly seen taking their share of the hardware in club events throughout this country and abroad, and either the short or long variant is a superb rally machine.

A larger-displacement, V-8 engine is the subject of a recurring rumor. A more likely possibility is a further development of the XK engine which, though approaching the end of its second decade, has tremendous latent potentialities.

While enthusiasts yearn for Jaguar to return to works-supported racing, Sir William Lyons is content, for the moment, with an annual production of some 30,000 cars in a wide variety. In July, 1966, Jaguar Cars Limited of Coventry merged with the British Motor Corporation. The eventual blend of outstanding engineering talent will almost certainly produce further sensational types before the end of this decade, with that "different breed of cat" called Jaguar continuing to be a car of amazing quality at a price that gives fine-car lovers more than their money's worth.

# SPECIFICATIONS Chapter 8

| | XK-E 3.8-Litre March 1961— | XK-E 4.2-Litre 1964— | XK-E 2+2 4.2-Litre 1966— |
|---|---|---|---|
| Bore, Stroke (mm.) | 87 x 106 | 92.07 x 106 | 92.07 x 106 |
| Displacement (c.c.) | 3781 | 4235 | 4235 |
| Compression ratio | 9.0 8.0 option | 9.0 8.0 option | 9.0 8.0 option |
| Carburetors | 3 S.U. HD.8 | 3 S.U. HD.8 | 3 S.U. HD.8 |
| Brake Horse-power @ RPM | 265 @ 5500 | 265 @ 5500 | 265 @ 5500 |
| Transmission | 4 Manual | 4 Manual | 4 Manual 3 Automatic |
| Rear axle ratios | 3.31 Manual 2.97 " 3.07 " 3.54 " | 3.31 Manual 3.07 " 3.54 " | 3.54 Manual 3.07 " 3.31 Automatic 2.88 " |
| Length overall (inches) | 175.3 | 175.3 | 184.5 |
| Width overall | 65.25 | 65.25 | 65.25 |
| Height overall | 48.1 Coupe 46.5 Roadster | 48.1 Coupe 46.5 Roadster | 50.12 |
| Tires | 15 x 6.40 | 15 x 6.40 | 15 x 6.40 |
| Wheelbase | 96 | 96 | 105 |
| Tread, front " rear | 50 50 | 50 50 | 50 50 |
| Curb weight (approx.) | 2600 up | 2600 up | 3000 up |

# JOSEPH H. WHERRY

was born in 1918 in Everett, Washington, and now lives with his wife, Bettye, and their four children in Santa Rosa, California. He is the author of many general and special interest magazine articles and ten books, and when "time permits, which it seldom does," likes to build airplane and railroad models to scale. A photographer as well as a writer, Mr. Wherry illustrates many of his own works. He has contributed to *Motor Trend* and *Road and Track* magazines, and from 1956 to 1958 was the Detroit editor of *Motor Trend*. With his interest in things automotive, it was natural for him to turn his skills to books on the subject. Among his published titles in this field are *Economy Car Blitz, Antique and Classic Cars,* and *The MG Story*. The last and *The Jaguar Story* by Mr. Wherry are books in Chilton's Sebring Series. *Automobiles of the World* is in preparation.